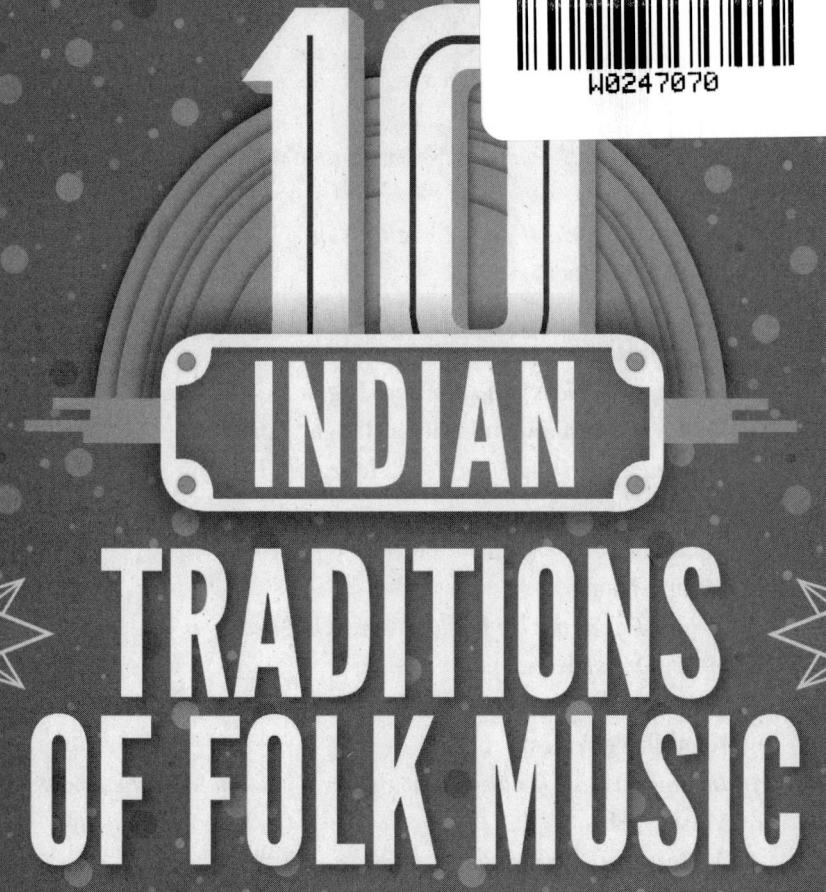

10

INDIAN

TRADITIONS OF FOLK MUSIC

THAT TELL OUR STORIES

MAMTA NAINY

Read more in the 10s series

10 INDIAN TRADITIONS OF FOLK MUSIC THAT TELL OUR STORIES

MAMTA NAINY

An imprint of Penguin Random House

For the countless keepers of India's folk music traditions,
who carry songs in their hearts and histories.

DUCKBILL BOOKS

Duckbill Books is an imprint of the Penguin Random House group of companies
whose addresses can be found at global.penguinrandomhouse.com

Published by Penguin Random House India Pvt. Ltd
4th Floor, Capital Tower 1, MG Road,
Gurugram 122 002, Haryana, India

Penguin
Random House
India

First published in Duckbill Books by Penguin Random House India 2025

ISBN 9780143465577

Typeset in Sitka by Digiultrabooks Pvt. Ltd
Printed at Replika Press Pvt. Ltd, India

www.penguin.co.in

MIX
Paper | Supporting
responsible forestry
FSC™ C016779

10

INTRODUCTION

On a late-summer evening, as dusk slowly settled over a prehistoric valley, the sky shifted in colour. A group of early humans sat beneath an ancient tree near a cluster of caves by a river meandering through the valley. A meadow grasshopper buzzed in a weed clump; a melodious cricket chirped in the grass; a cicada filled the valley with its shrill, sustained songs; and a lone bird serenaded with its joyous tunes of homecoming. Imitating the sounds they heard, the early humans joined this grand orchestra and the musical extravaganza took an entirely different turn!

Beginnings have often been a matter of contestation—there is no history still that can establish the beginning of time. The same holds true for the origin of music. Though it would be fair to say that if one thinks of the history of humanity as one day, then music has existed since the dawn of that day. There is no way of knowing who sang the first song, whistled the first tune, or made the first rhythmic sounds that resembled what we know today as music. But undoubtedly it happened thousands of years ago.

Early humans may have sung as long as they could speak, though they likely did not croon full-length songs. Instead, it is conjectured that they made simpler vocal sounds, mostly imitations of sounds in nature and shared similar tonality, patterns and repetitions to those sounds. When the wind howled, they howled back; when it rained, they hummed along; and when they hunted, they mimicked animal sounds. According to historians, this earliest form of music, called the prehistoric era of music, was produced between 50,000 BCE and 4000 BCE and was primarily vocal—the early humans either hummed, whistled, clicked or grunted.

Soon, early humans realized that their bodies could become instruments to create music and were mediums for performance. They created rhythm by clapping, pounding, thumping, walking and running. With rituals at the heart of their song and dance, early humans sang prayers and made offerings to the elements of nature. Eventually, they invented musical instruments to produce the sounds they could not—pipes and flutes mimicked the wind, whistles and rattles imitated birds and drums and gongs amplified the sound of the heartbeat. How do we know this? Through numerous archaeological finds of bone flutes, pipes and whistles—objects fashioned from animal bones that are meant to be blown into. One of the oldest bone flutes, found by archaeologists in a Slovenian cave and dating back at least 45,000 years, is made from the femur bone of a bear cub. It even has holes punched into its sides, allowing the musical pitch to be raised or lowered by covering one or more of these holes!

Over time, music transformed as it changed hands (or mouths). With the development of written language in 4000 BCE, music evolved from random sounds and pitches to conscious melodies and patterns. As it grew more complex, people began to codify it. Over centuries and across civilizations, musical systems flourished within various cultures, each with its own rules, methods and techniques that resonated with established practices. You could think of these musical systems as grand architectures that follow certain imaginative patterns, an understanding of which was passed down in a highly structured teaching-learning process. Thus, the formal, performance-driven tradition of classical music was born.

Before the evolution of classical music, another tradition grew from the same rhythmic roots but was not tied to formal training or an audience. This tradition was born out of the everyday life of ordinary people as a source of entertainment, religious, cultural or emotional expression and it is what we call folk music. Deeply embedded in the storytelling tradition, folk music translates a community's oral narratives into songs that are carried across generations of anonymous musicians. These songs weave together various themes and experiences in simple language and are sung to break the monotony of life. They draw inspiration from the daily rhythms of life such as the sound of the grinding stone, the drone of a spinning wheel and the beat of the horse's hooves.

In a country as diverse as India, there are as many folk music traditions as there are languages. Each tradition offers songs for every season and reason—spring and winter, hardship and celebration, love and loss, hope and sorrow, endurance and solidarity and songs purely for joy! Passed down through generations, these songs capture the essence of life, weaving together communal bonds and cultural rituals.

However, like all cultural expressions, music is

influenced by social structures. Caste, gender and class have often shaped who sings, who listens and what stories are told. In many communities, certain musical roles were traditionally reserved for specific castes. Women, despite being central to the creation and performance of folk music, often faced restrictions on when and where they could sing. Yet, within these constraints, some powerful musical expressions have emerged.

This book explores ten distinct folk music traditions from across India, each offering a unique perspective on the cultural fabric of its community. While no single selection can capture the full spectrum of India's diverse folk music, these ten provide a glimpse into its richness. Like culture itself, folk music is dynamic and ever-evolving as it adapts to the changing needs of its audience and context. Through these pages, we will explore the vibrant stories of the communities giving voice to the many Indias.

LISTENING LISTS

Words can only go so far in describing a piece of music; it is far better to listen to it. At the end of each chapter, you will find a listening list of recommended YouTube links that represent the folk music tradition discussed. While these recommendations are a great starting point, they are not exhaustive. Keep your mind and ears open, and let these folk tunes take over!

SONGS OF SEPARATION

The Bidesia Migration Music of Bihar

It is a morning like any other. There is the usual hustle-bustle at the Darbhanga railway station. The Bihar Sampark Kranti Express is about to leave the platform. The general compartment is packed beyond capacity. Leaving their families behind, hundreds from Bihar's villages embark on uncertain journeys to the bulging cities in search of employment.

What would it take for you to pack up a few of your possessions and move to a city far from home? The decision to leave behind your home, family and friends for an unknown city is never easy. The uncertainty is daunting—will the new city welcome you? Will you find work and a place to live? Will you be able to learn the unfamiliar language? These are just a few of the challenges migrants face. Yet thousands of people embark on long, arduous journeys to urban centres every day, driven by the hope of a better life and livelihood.

Many of these migrants come from Bhojpur, a cultural entity that transcends political borders and includes parts of eastern Uttar Pradesh, western Bihar and northwestern Jharkhand, where the Bhojpuri language is spoken. This region has a long history of migration due to limited local opportunities, typically restricted to fieldwork or daily wage labour. To secure a stable income for their families, people from Bhojpur often journey to distant places in search of better prospects.

The invisible hands of these migrant workers clean streets, run factories, construct roads and houses and essentially help build megacities, but they seldom find social acceptance. While struggling to make a living, they also face the hardships of city life, including a lack of affordable housing and amenities. And back home, their families spend years waiting for their return. How then do migrant workers and their families anchor themselves in this state of separation and constant uncertainty? One way is through music.

The folk music of Bihar is a repository of the lived realities of its people—their hopes and aspirations, pains and sorrows, struggles and stories. Over time, it has responded to the issues of migration by giving a distinct voice to the anxieties of migrant workers and their families through a unique Bhojpuri folk music tradition called *bidesia*, a term that loosely translates to an affectionate form of address given to someone who has travelled to a foreign land.

BONDED LABOUR AND BIDESIA

It was the year 1834. Most houses were illuminated by earthen lamps and palanquins and horse-drawn carriages were more common on the streets than the smoke-breathing cars and buses. The British ruled India, exerting influence not only over trade and commerce but also over the socio-economic policies of the country.

Under one such British policy of indentured labour—
designed to address labour shortages in British colonies by
contracting Indian workers under specific terms—thirty-six
impoverished men and women from villages across the
present-day Indian states of Uttar Pradesh, Bihar and
Bengal signed a contract with George Charles Arbuthnot
of Hunter-Arbuthnot & Company, a major British trading
company and were herded on to a boat on the Hooghly
river and taken to a sail-ship called *Atlas*. These indentured
labourers were cooped up in the dark and damp underdeck
of the ship carrying a large rice cargo. The ship was bound
for an island called Marich Desh (the land of the magician
Maricha from the epic of Ramayana and present-day
Mauritius).

Mauritius was first discovered by the Portuguese in
the fourteenth century and colonized by the Dutch and
French and finally by the British in 1814. With the abolition
of slavery in the United States in 1833–34 threatening
to cause a workforce shortage, the British desperately
needed cheap, mobile labour to work in the flourishing
sugarcane plantations. The only source of cheap labour
that the British could think of was India, where there was
no dearth of poor people from oppressed castes who were
looking for new means of livelihood.

So, the British devised the system of 'indenture'.
Frequent famines, political instability following the end of
the Mughal era and British-controlled opium cultivation
which rendered fertile lands unfit for farming, led many
Indian farm workers, particularly from Bihar and Bengal,
into severe debt. They were lured—tricked and bullied

even—by the Indian middlemen into signing contracts they did not fully understand, agreeing to work in British plantations overseas. The workers were bonded for a minimum of five years and worked under harsh conditions. To safeguard their commercial interests, the British effectively replaced slavery with another form of bondage—indentured labour—at virtually no cost!

ACROSS THE KAALA PAANI

To work on the plantations, Indian workers had to overcome the deeply ingrained taboo of crossing Kaala Paani or Black Waters. Many Hindus believed that crossing the sea would result in a loss of caste, a status that was nearly impossible to restore. Most of the workers who agreed to labour overseas on these plantations belonged to the oppressed castes, at the bottom of the caste hierarchy.

For the thirty-six men and women on the *Atlas*, the perilous three-month-long journey to Mauritius meant an escape from debt and poverty. Inadvertently, they became participants in India's earliest recorded large-scale labour movement, part of the British's Great Experiment of substituting slavery with indentured labour. Over the next eighty years, till 1916, five lakh Indians would make similar voyages to various British colonies such as Fiji, Jamaica, Guyana, Suriname, Trinidad and Tobago, to toil in foreign lands. The name given to them was Girmitiyas, derived from a Hindi word *girmit*, a corruption of the English word 'agreement' or the contract they had signed.

HOW SLAVERY SHAPED COLONIAL FARMS

Between 1500 and 1800, European powers, such as the Portuguese, Spanish, British and Dutch, forcibly transported thousands and thousands of enslaved Africans to the Americas, including the British colonies that would eventually become the United States. In the Southern colonies, with scarce European workers and frequent Native American resistance, plantation owners increasingly relied on the brutal system of slavery to cultivate lucrative crops like cotton and tobacco. This dark chapter significantly impacted the development of colonial agriculture.

At the plantations, the workers had to rebuild their lives and identities under extremely punishing conditions with next to no means. They were housed in overcrowded 'coolie' barracks, many of which had served as quarters for formally enslaved Africans. With hardly any toilets and human waste piling up in the open, disease was rampant and medical care was scarce. The workers endured heavy workloads and were paid a pittance—men were paid twelve annas (around seventy-five paise) and women were paid nine annas (around fifty-four paise) daily. To top it all, the workers felt deeply homesick. The only way to communicate with their families was through letters, which often did not even reach their recipients.

One of the few things that connected the workers to their homeland and families was their songs. In the mid-nineteenth century, there emerged a folk music tradition that not only allowed the workers to express their anguish at being transported to *bides* (foreign land), mostly against their will and their pain of separation from their loved ones but also became an instrument of resistance against the plantation hardships. These songs described how Indian recruiters and middlemen deceived them with promises of a better life in a magical land, while also reflecting on the loneliness of the workers and their families. This music, rooted in the distinct folk genres popular in Bihar and Uttar Pradesh—such as *biraha* (songs of longing), *jaatsar* (songs sung while grinding grains), *chaiti* (songs of spring)—served as a balm for them at the end of a long day of toil.

One example of an indentured song sung by the women migrants goes as follows:

> *Bholi bhali dekh arkati bharmaya ho,*
> *Kalkatta par jao pach sal re bidesia . . .*
> *Dipuwa ma laye pakadayo kagaduwa ho,*
> *Angutha lagay din hay re bidesia . . .*
> *Pal ke jahajuwa me roye dhoye baithi ho,*
> *Kaise hoi Kaala Paani paar re bidesia.*
>
> [A recruiter saw my innocence and tricked me,
> Into going beyond Calcutta for five years, O migrant . . .
> He brought me into a depot to sign a contract,
> And took my fingerprints on it, O migrant . . .
> I sat crying on the sailing ship,
> Wondering how I crossed the Black Waters, O migrant.]

CHUTNEY MUSIC

Over time, the native songs brought by indentured workers to British plantations, especially in the Caribbean, absorbed various local musical influences and gave rise to a vibrant fusion genre known as chutney music. Here's how to whip up some chutney music:

1. Start with Bhojpuri folk songs sung during harvests, weddings, or as bhajans (devotional songs).

2. Combine with a smattering of Caribbean English for a smooth mix.

3. Whisk together the sounds of the dholak and harmonium with the steel pan and guitar.

4. Add roughly chopped chunks of Afro-Caribbean styles like calypso, reggae and soca.

5. Sprinkle with creole (mixed) accents.

6. Garnish with spicy beats.

Your flavourful fusion genre, perfect for lingering on the music appreciator's palate, is ready to be served.

THE SHAKESPEARE OF BHOJPURI

At the beginning of the twentieth century, as nationalist fervour swept across India, the system of indentured labour came under attack. Many people came forward to lead massive campaigns against the colonial policy. Newspapers and magazines such as *Saraswati*, *Vishal Bharat* and *Pravasi* were launched with the specific aim of raising awareness about the injustices faced by Indians working on plantations. During this period, numerous novels and short stories were written around the theme of departure, while songs, plays, dance and art gave voice to the anxieties of the workers and their families. This led to the evolution of bidesia culture. Several folk theatre artists, such as Guddar Rai, Sundari Bai, Dunia Bai and Ramsakal Pathak 'Dwijram', contributed to this culture, but one artist in particular helped to crystallize bidesia as a distinct form of folk music. Known as the Shakespeare of Bhojpuri, his name was Bhikhari Thakur.

A playwright, poet, singer, actor, dancer and social activist, Bhikhari Thakur hailed from the small village of Kutubpur in Saran district of Bihar. He belonged to a community of barbers, which was ranked low in the hierarchy of India's complicated caste system. When his village was ravaged by a terrible famine, Thakur migrated to Calcutta (present-day Kolkata) in search of livelihood, leaving his young bride behind. In Calcutta, he was exposed to city life as well as popular folk theatre forms such as jatra and Ramlila. He also visited Puri and Bhubaneswar, where he was captivated by recitals of Tulsidas's *Ramcharitmanas*. After a few years of struggle, Thakur made some money, but he longed for home. He returned to his village and started performing Ramlila. However, he soon faced strong opposition from upper-caste Hindus who believed that people from lower castes were not allowed to perform such an important religious text. Undeterred, Thakur formed a theatre group and began writing and directing his own plays in his mother tongue, Bhojpuri.

One of Thakur's most popular plays, born from the prevailing social issues of the time, was a musical called *Bidesia*. The play narrated the pain of migration, particularly from the perspective of a newly wedded wife whose husband had migrated to the city—a theme that resonated deeply with Bhojpuri audiences. At that time, since women were not allowed to perform publicly, men cross-dressed as women to portray female characters. Bhikhari Thakur composed the songs for the play, drawing from popular folk tunes such as biraha, *barahmasa, kajri* and *chaiti*. The play featured six songs about migration—one of which, 'Bhave Naahin Bhavanan, Ho Ram, Videsh Gavanvan' (I do not care for palaces, oh Ram, my beloved has gone to a foreign land), became immensely popular. Although the play is now over a hundred years old, its songs remain widely recognizable and are still sung by people in the region today.

LAUNDA NAACH

Naach, also known as *launda naach*, is a vibrant folk theatre tradition from the Bhojpur region. Performed by men in female roles, it captures a range of local issues and emotions. Originally, part of various folk forms, launda naach's most prominent form became *Bidesia* by Bhikhari Thakur. Although earlier forms existed, Thakur played a crucial role in shaping and popularizing this tradition. Today, the term 'bidesia' is often used interchangeably with 'launda naach', highlighting its central theme of migration and its cultural significance.

Owing to the popularity of Thakur's play, other folk theatre groups also started making use of this style of theatre and, before long, bidesia became a popular folk musical style of the Bhojpuri region.

TANSEN MEETS BHAGAT SINGH

Mahendra Mishra, a key influence on Bhikhari Thakur, popularized the *purvi* genre of Bhojpuri music that inspired many of Thakur's compositions. Born in 1886, Mishra was a poet, musician, wrestler and freedom fighter. He excelled in music and mythological narratives, mastering various instruments and composing songs that resonated with folk musicians, including Thakur. During the Swadeshi movement, Mishra also contributed to India's independence struggle by covertly printing fake currency notes to fund freedom fighters.

THE 'WOMEN'S' SONGS

As a result of the protests, the migration of Indian workers to foreign lands officially stopped in 1917, but a new wave of internal migration gripped Bihar. With few livelihood options available in the villages, many agricultural workers began migrating to cities such as Kolkata, Delhi and Mumbai. In these urban centres, they found work as rickshaw pullers and autorickshaw or taxi drivers. These new circumstances were reflected in the folk songs of the region, many of which were from the perspective of women.

For centuries, bidesia folk songs have served as a vital outlet for Bhojpuri-speaking women, allowing them to express what they often cannot speak aloud. Rooted in daily negotiations, these songs often articulate women's anger, insecurities, frustrations and desires, going beyond merely lamenting their absent husbands. There are, in fact, many bidesia songs that raise important questions about caste hierarchies, social morality, domestic violence and power dynamics within the family and the challenges of single parenting.

Sisterhood is also an important theme in these songs, as shared desires and common experiences among women foster a collective voice. The rhythms of bidesia songs are often synchronized with daily chores such as grinding grains and pounding with a pestle, showcasing how women's labour contributes to the creation of any folk culture.

Bidesia songs enable women to actively resist social oppression, expressing their unique voices through everyday acts of resistance. These songs, therefore, sing of women's agency and define their own ideas of identity and independence.

THE SOUNDS OF THE TIMES

During the 2020 coronavirus pandemic, a nationwide lockdown was swiftly imposed. Throngs of migrants were thrown on to the streets, forced to leave the cities they had been living and working in for decades. They walked for several days to reach their distant homes. Their journeys were reflections of the inherent disparity in our country—the callousness and neglect towards the people who build our homes and roads and form the very backbone of our working class.

During the pandemic, the migrants were not leaving behind their homeland but were, in fact, going back to their villages and families, but emotional anguish and sense of displacement was the same. These emotions, too, found resonance in the bidesia songs that captured the pain of ordinary people caught in extraordinary circumstances. They became as relevant (or perhaps more relevant) as they were when they were first sung.

MIGRATION MUSIC ACROSS INDIA

The relationship between music and memory is powerful. Music evokes memories, transporting us to another place and time. Perhaps that is why many different communities across the world have used music to tell their migration stories and feel connected with their homelands. Two such notable Indian music traditions are:

KATHU PATTU: The 1970s oil boom in the Gulf spurred a major wave of migration from Kerala, which now has the largest Indian diaspora in the region. A notable aspect of the Malayali diaspora and their families back home is *kathu pattu* (letter songs). Written in Arabi Malayalam, which uses Arabic letters to represent Malayalam words, these songs are popular among the Muslim migrants from northern Malabar. They often reflect the letters exchanged between migrants and their families left behind.

SIDDI DHAMAAL: From the eleventh to the seventeenth century, Islamic invaders and Portuguese colonizers transported many Africans to India as enslaved people. They primarily settled in Gujarat, Karnataka, Maharashtra, Goa and Andhra Pradesh, and are collectively known as the Siddis. Despite their diverse tribal origins, they preserved African socio-cultural traditions while adapting to local cultures. One notable result of this cultural blend is the *dhamaal* tradition of the Siddis in Gujarat. This spiritual music and dance form is performed in memory of Siddi saints and reflects a fusion of Sufi and African musical practices.

Today, these songs echo the bidesia of the old and keep the memory of the past alive while also singing of social and cultural interactions that define present times. Earlier, these songs sang of the awaiting letters and now, the letters might have been replaced with words like '*mobile-wa*', but the essence of these songs remains intact—the immense social price that migrants and their families have to pay.

The exact origin of many of these songs is rarely known and they largely survive on memory and repetition, but they carry a common thread of experiences—a thread flexible enough to incorporate new forms of expressing collective imagination and experiences. And as these songs get passed down from one generation to the next, they continue to sing of the times, of the many journeys that have been taken and of those too that are being taken this very moment.

LISTENING LIST:

Search words: Bhojpuri Folk Music, Bidesia Songs, Chutney Music, Bhikhari Thakur

1. A poignant Bhojpuri folk song by Gopal Maurya, which reflects on the experiences of indentured migration.
   https://www.youtube.com/watch?v=d4UBjB6WB5w

2. A Bhojpuri folk singer captures the pain of a woman whose husband has migrated to a far-off land. This song was originally written by Bhikhari Thakur.
   https://www.youtube.com/watch?v=WUeN5TrD-20

3. The Bhojpuri artist Kalpana Patowary's vibrant chutney performance at the Paddy Fields Folk Fusion Music Festival 2017.
   https://www.youtube.com/watch?v=dU5PZ7mHL6Q

4. A traditional Bhojpuri song that captures the heartfelt emotions of longing and separation.
   https://www.youtube.com/watch?v=U-qEpWNIRog

5. A stirring Bhojpuri folk song, capturing themes of patriotism.
   https://www.youtube.com/watch?v=PScrj68PigY

SONGS OF MAGICAL LANDS AND EARTHY WISDOM

The Gathas and Kathas of the Manganiyar-Langas of Rajasthan

Long, long ago, the kingdom of Pugal in Rajasthan was ravaged by a terrible famine. In the fields where heavy and golden harvest should have rustled, there were only tens of thousands of fissures. One by one, the people of Pugal left their homes in search of greener pastures. Finally, Pingal, the king of Pugal, too, left his kingdom with his family.

After a long journey, Pingal and his family reached the rich and bountiful kingdom of Narwar. When the king of Narwar, Nal, learned of the arrival of the royal family of Pugal, he welcomed them warmly and offered them a place to stay at his palace for as long as they wished.

The king and queen of Pugal had a daughter named Maruni, or Maru, and the king and queen of Narwar had a son named Dhola. One day, the queen of Pugal saw the toddler prince of Narwar playing in the palace garden and thought that he would be an ideal match for her daughter. The proposal was put before the king and queen of Narwar, who were happy to accept it. Dhola and Maru were *married. Soon after the wedding, news of heavy rains in Pugal reached Pingal. The king, the queen and little Maru returned home.*

As time passed, Dhola and Maru grew up. Their marriage was all but forgotten until one night Maru dreamed of Dhola. Meanwhile, the Narwar prince had married Malwani, the princess of Malwa. Maru's many attempts to send word to Dhola were met with failure. When nothing else worked, Maru sent a group of folk singers to Narwar to perform songs composed by the princess in Raag Maru. Amidst the stormy rains, the singers sang these melodious songs which triggered the prince's memory and reminded him of Maru. Determined to right all wrong, Dhola travelled to Pugal and after many twists and turns, he was finally united with Maru.

Star-crossed lovers and vicious villains, brave princes and warrior princesses, benevolent ghosts and clever seths, faithful horses and eccentric camels—the world of Rajasthani folklore has long been populated with enchanting characters and earthy wisdom. 'Dhola Maru Ra Doha' (the ballad of Dhola and Maru), is one such epic romance that has drifted across the desert dunes of Rajasthan for generations. It has been sung as *gathas* and *kathas*—the little-known ballad and epic traditions of Rajasthan—by the itinerant Manganiyar and Langa folk singers.

THE BARDS OF THE DESERTS

Heirs to the rich narrative musical traditions of Rajasthan, the minstrels and balladeers of the Manganiyar-Langa communities hail from the heart of the Thar region of western Rajasthan, mainly from the districts of Barmer and Jaisalmer and the villages along the border of Pakistan. For centuries, they have survived on the hereditary patronage of local nobility—the wealthy cattle breeders and landowners of the region.

Both the Manganiyar and Langa communities are of the Muslim faith, but the patrons of the Manganiyars are largely Hindus, while those of the Langas are Muslims. Traditionally, on important social occasions such as births, marriages, deaths, festivals and *kutcheris* (musical gatherings), the musicians are expected to perform at the homes of their patrons. From their extensive repertoire of music, which ranges from ballads about the kings and the queens to lifecycle songs to harvest melodies and hymns of devotion, the musicians belt out song after song to suit the occasion. Sung in the Marwari or Sindhi language to an indigenous system of *ragas* (musical modes), the folk music tradition of the Manganiyar-Langa survives largely through memory and oral transmission.

The word 'Manganiyar' means 'those who ask for alms'. There are many legends surrounding the origin of the community. One such legend links them to the birth of the grandsons of Prophet Muhammad. It is believed that when Hasan and Husain were born to Bibi Fatima, the daughter of Prophet Muhammad, a *mirasi* (hereditary folk singer) named Mangan came to the prophet's house and sang a *sehra* (congratulatory song), in honour of the newborns. In immense appreciation for Mangan's music, Bibi Fatima gave him the *haar* (necklace) she was wearing. She also blessed him, saying that many generations after him would hold a special place in the courts of the kings and nobles. The singer was given the name 'Manganhaar' and over time, his descendants came to be known as Manganiyars.

Some scholars suggest that Manganiyar originated from the word '*mahaguniar*', which roughly translates to 'those with supreme talent'. The Manganiyars are said to have originally belonged to the Mirasi community of folklore tellers and traditional singers in Sindh (now in Pakistan). When Sindh was invaded by the Arab military commander Muhammad Ibn al-Qasim in 712 CE, they migrated to western Rajasthan, where they were employed by Rajput courts and local nobles.

The term 'Langa', on the other hand, means 'the song giver'. The oral traditions of the Langa community attest to a Hindu past and it is believed the Langas converted from Hinduism to Islam in the fifteenth century. The story goes that two Rajput brothers once lived together. One day, the younger brother was crossing a neighbourhood madrasa when he saw a musical procession. Mesmerized by the music, he followed the procession. Once the singers stopped, he requested them to teach him their music. He is believed to have later accepted Islam and became a wandering minstrel. The descendants of this man are known as the Langas, meaning those who sing and spread music.

The Langas migrated from Sindh and settled in Baranwa village of the Barmer district. Over the years, they moved to other parts of Rajasthan as well. At present, the majority of the Langa population is distributed in the Barmer, Jaisalmer and Jodhpur districts of Rajasthan.

THE 'JAJMANI' SYSTEM OF PATRONAGE

One of the most fundamental aspects of the Manganiyar-Langa folk music tradition is a system of local patronage called the *jajmani pratha*. Each musician's family has at least one *jajman* (patron). The relationship between a musician's family and that of the patron's spans many generations, so a musician's family is associated not just with the individual patron but with the entire lineage. Traditionally, the jajmani system has been the main source of sustenance for the Manganiyar-Langa musicians and they earn in cash or kind (money, food grains, land, livestock and even gold) by singing for the patrons.

As the Manganiyar-Langa musicians owe allegiance to the same patron for generations, they are also responsible for maintaining their genealogical records, sometimes going back eighteen generations across many centuries! Remarkably, these genealogical records are memorized and orally passed down through generations. The communities have specific types of musical compositions called *subhraj* that recount the family history of the jajmans and are sung on social occasions. In addition to the subhraj, the musicians also sing songs collectively known as *bakhaan,* which praise the jajman, his character, ancestry and—without fail—his generosity. The relationship between the musicians and patrons is so important that musicians tend to settle in the areas where their respective jajmans live or move to.

Because the Langas are exclusively attached to Muslim patrons and the Manganiyars mainly to Rajput ones, their musical styles are shaped by the tastes and traditions of their respective benefactors. While their repertoires overlap, each community also has songs that are uniquely their own. Both the communities sing in the same dialect and believe that their music is a way of life—so much so that it is said that when a baby is born in these communities, he or she cries to the notes of music. Just as the mother tongue or indigenous vocational skills such as weaving or pottery are passed down, Langa and Manganiyar children are initiated into singing from a very young age. Unlike Indian classical music, however, their musical training does not occur in a formal environment. The children, especially boys, start accompanying their fathers to the patrons' houses to sing during social occasions. Through these long, free-flowing performances, the community's repertoire of songs is revised and passed on to the next generation.

Apart from the songs associated with feasts and festivities, the Manganiyar-Langa musicians also sing songs about the different seasons, such as *barsalo* (monsoon songs), *unalo* (summer songs), *basant* (spring songs) and *siyalo* (winter songs). A popular rain song from the Manganiyar-Langa tradition goes:

Jhirmir jhirmir,
Jhirmar jhirmir . . .
Balam ji mahra,
Jhirmir barse meh.
Jhirmir jhirmir mehuda barse,
O piya ji base pardes . . .
[Softly, softly,
Gently, gently,
O beloved one,
The rain drizzles.
The raindrops descend,
While you are in a distant land.]

The Manganiyar-Langa repertoire also includes ballads of epic romances like Moomal-Mahendra, Umar-Marvi and Sassi-Punnu, Sindhi-Sufi *kalams* (songs) and Hindu bhajans and compositions by poet-saints like Kabir, Mirabai, Surdas and Dadu Dayal. Their musical tradition, entirely oral, encompasses at least a thousand different songs. Each song begins with a *doha* (poetic couplet), which is usually a snippet taken from the main tale. Typically, the performances are occasion-driven and the musicians do a lot of spontaneous improvisation while performing the songs.

A TREASURE HUNT WITH A DIFFERENCE

Traditionally, the Manganiyars played *kakadi* (a musical treasure hunt) during birth ceremonies and weddings at their patrons' homes. In this game, musicians, grouped in fives or sixes, would sit in the middle of the courtyard, surrounded by members of the patron's family. Before the performance began, the musicians would hide a small object in the patron's house. The family members then had to find it, guided by musical clues.

Unlike a typical treasure hunt, kakadi used different ragas as clues. The six main ragas of Manganiyar folk music—Maru, Sorath, Dhani, Soobh, Megh Malhar and Goond Malhar—corresponded to the four cardinal directions (north, south, east and west) and the vertical dimensions (up and down).

This game demanded significant musical skill from both the musicians and the patrons. The musicians had to expertly transition between ragas to guide the patrons toward the hidden object, while the patrons needed to understand the ragas to translate them into correct directions. As musical expertise wanes, this game is gradually fading from memory.

THE MUSICAL INNOVATORS

The full-throated voices of the Manganiyar-Langa musicians, which can sweep across miles even without a microphone, are usually accompanied by the sounds of beautiful instruments. Often, these instruments are handmade by highly skilled local craftspeople using naturally available materials such as different types of wood, reed, animal skin and bones. Most children in the community start playing these instruments, which are readily available in their homes, at an early age and become adept at playing multiple instruments as they grow up.

One of these instruments that has become synonymous with the Manganiyar community is the *kamaicha*. This instrument is so intrinsically tied to the Manganiyar identity that a popular saying in the region goes, 'Where there is a kamaicha, there is a Manganiyar.' Among the oldest of stringed instruments, the kamaicha has not undergone any structural changes over the last five hundred years—it is still created and played the way it has always been. The kamaicha is a bowed lute with seventeen strings and its body is made of seasoned mango wood and goat skin. It is played using a wide bow called *gaj*, made from the wood of sheesham tree. A difficult instrument to master, the kamaicha gently traces the contours of the singer's voice and produces a deep, resonating sound. In recent years, however, many young singers have switched to the harmonium as an accompanying instrument, as they haven't learned the art of playing kamaicha, which requires long, rigorous training.

While the kamaicha provides depth to Manganyari music, the khartal and dholak infuse it with rhythm and energy. The dholak is a double-headed barrel drum used for rhythmic accompaniment while the khartals are hand-held wooden castanets that are not connected but are clapped together to produce rapid rhythms. Sometimes, a wind percussion instrument called the morchang is also used. Held against the mouth, the *morchang* resembles a Jew's harp and produces a twangy sound when a little metal tongue at its end is plucked.

The Langas are divided into two classes based on the instruments they play—the Sarangiyas and the Surnaiyas. The Sarangiya Langas sing to the music of *sarangi*, a string instrument that is also sometimes used by the Manganiyars. The Surnaiyas, on the other hand, play a rare string instrument called the *surinda*, of which there are only about fifteen pieces surviving in India today.

FROM LOCAL TO GLOBAL

If you have ever watched a group of five or six men in white dhoti-kurtas and bright, oversized tie-dye turbans sitting in a semicircle and singing 'Kesariya Balam Aavo Ne Padharo Mhare Des' or 'Nimbooda-Nimbooda' on a reality singing show, then chances are you've witnessed a Manganiyar-Langa performance. The music of the Manganiyars and the Langas was relatively obscure until Komal Kothari single-handedly put these powerful musical traditions on the world map, where they now enthral global audiences through live performances and movie songs.

An ethnomusicologist, folklorist and unrivalled expert in desert music, Komal Kothari, or Komalda as he was fondly called, started a monthly literary journal called *Prerna*, along with a close friend and one of the foremost Rajasthani writers, Vijaydan Detha in 1953, which set itself the task of writing about a new Rajasthani folk song each month.

In 1958, Komalda became the first secretary of the Sangeet Natak Akademi in Jodhpur where he began to explore the Manganiyar-Langa music traditions. He travelled extensively throughout Rajasthan, documenting their songs. Realizing that these cultures were slowly becoming endangered, he decided to make recordings of their music. During one such attempt in 1960 to record the songs of singer Antar Khan Manganiyar in Jodhpur, Komalda was readying his vintage tape recorder when he turned around to find the singer sprinting away! Komalda chased him over a long distance and finally, with great effort, caught up. When he asked Antar Khan why he had run away, the singer explained that he feared the machine would swallow his voice, leaving him unable to sing!

Over the next few years, Komalda worked to assuage the community's misgivings and recorded many Manganiyar-Langa songs. In 1960, he co-founded Rupayan Sansthan, an institution dedicated to preserving Rajasthan's folk arts. In the 1970s, he introduced these music traditions to the world by ensuring that folk artists found a place in performance circuits. The winter years of his life, too, were spent building a unique living museum of folk culture and oral traditions of Rajasthan, the Arna Jharna Museum, located in the village of Moklawas in Jodhpur.

Today, many Manganiyar-Langa musicians have brought their rich musical traditions to a global stage, earning widespread recognition through Hindi film music and television shows. Among these artists, Anwar Khan stands out for his contributions to the documentary *Pipasa* with the song 'Paanido Barsa De' and the film *Dhanak* with 'Mehandi'. Mame Khan is celebrated for his tracks 'Baawre' from *Luck by Chance* and 'Baaghi Re' from *Sonchiriya*. Sarwar Khan and Sartaz Khan are also notable for their performance of 'Haanikaarak Bapu' from *Dangal*. These artists have played a pivotal role in introducing Manganiyar-Langa music to a broader audience.

THE WOMEN MUSICIANS

The women musicians of the Manganiyar-Langa communities have always been involved in singing and composing music—in fact, they are the first music teachers of their children. Historically, women from these communities performed within their own circles or for women patrons. However, during the nineteenth century, Victorian ideas of gendered public and private lives began to influence local attitudes, leading to a decline in public performances by women. The communities began to internalize these ideas, perceiving women singing in public as a threat to their social status.

As a result, the Manganiyar-Langa music tradition became largely male-dominated. Despite this, a few women from the community have defied social norms and pursued their passion for music. One such pioneer was Rukma Bai, the first woman from the community to perform publicly in the modern era.

Known as the Nightingale of the Manganiyars, Rukma Bai was born in Barmer and afflicted with polio at an early age. A few years after marriage, her husband abandoned her due to her physical handicap. With three young children to take care of and recurrent drought that killed her cattle, she was in dire straits when Komal Kothari, who had heard her beautiful voice, encouraged her to perform in concerts. Everyone in her village tried to dissuade her, but Rukma Bai remained resolute.

When Rukma Bai first accepted the offer to sing on stage, she was ostracized by highly conservative community and was forced to live in virtual exile for two years. Her persistence paid off as she gained fame through performances around the world, leading her community to accept her. A staunch advocate for women's rights, Rukma Bai became one of the best-known voices of Rajasthan. Her courage inspired several other women musicians from the community, such as Maangi Bai, Halima Bai, Akla Bai and Dariya Bai, who are now reclaiming their space on stage.

CHRONICLERS OF A CULTURE

Songs are used by cultures worldwide as powerful tools to remember their ancestors and tell stories. The Manganiyar-Langas, too, are bearers of this tradition. Even today, they sing these songs, dance to them, collect them and belong to them. As chroniclers of their culture, they uphold the narratives of tradition, history, customs, language, society and geography across generations.

The Manganiyar-Langa music tradition has adapted and woven itself into the fabric of contemporary realities. Performances have moved from durbars and courtyards to auditoriums and arenas and the audience has shifted from local nobility to urban intelligentsia, in addition to the traditional rural gatherings.

Despite this, the tradition is at risk of fading due to a lack of proper support systems for these artists. While some musicians have gained visibility through reality TV shows and movies, many still live in remote villages and perform only for their jajmans. With only a few aging patrons left in Rajasthan who know and appreciate the gathas and kathas, the Manganiyar-Langa repertoire is constantly shrinking.

What remains crucial for the survival of this folk music tradition is that their precious songs continue to be sung and heard. Only when we discover these songs and pass them on can we truly understand the treasure troves of our nation's diverse histories and make sure that our stories do not just survive but flourish.

LISTENING LIST:

Search Words: Manganiyar Songs, Langa Songs, Rajasthani Folk Music, Anwar Khan Manganiyar, Rukma Bai Manganiyar, The Manganiyar Seduction, Dhola-Maru

1. A bhajan sung by the Manganiyar musician Anwar Khan and his group.
   https://www.youtube.com/watch?v=XPZAipxLe7Y

2. A song performed by a group of Langa children at the World Sufi Spirit Festival 2015.
   https://www.youtube.com/watch?v=45BZQeOA878

3. A field recording of Rukma Bai, the first woman Manganiyar singer in the modern era to perform publicly.
   https://www.youtube.com/watch?v=VBbC_iWUSQQ

4. The ballad of Dhola and Maru.
   https://www.youtube.com/watch?v=_2GrDLvVI1o

5. 'The Manganiyar Seduction', a theatrical concert directed by Roysten Abel, featuring musicians from three generations of Manganiyars performing in a thirty-six-windowed 'jewel box'.
   https://www.youtube.com/watch?v=YvKsrqCwyGQ

SONGS OF THE PEOPLE'S HISTORIANS

The Ladishah Ballads of Kashmir

1954. Wathoora village, Budgam district, Kashmir.

It was time for work. Gulzar Ahmed, or Gul, wore his pheran and headed for the chowk, the main square of the village. He navigated through the crowds, past the walnut artefact shops, the kebab vendors fanning their charcoal embers and the rugmakers plying their wares until he found a quiet spot for himself.

He took out his dhukri, *a rod-like instrument with thin metal rings and rolled his fingers over it to announce his arrival.*

Asalaam alaiqum ladishah aaw,

Ruth kanchan tohi gar soe chaw.

[The ladishah has arrived wishing you well.

Come, listen to the tales he is here to tell.]

A big crowd gathered. Gul called out a blessing, raised his hand and began singing the tale of the times. The new prime minister of Kashmir, who did not command

*popular support, had introduced a fleet of low-fare buses
to encourage tourism to the Valley—something that people
everywhere, from the masjids to the plazas to the streets,
had been talking about. Gul began:*

> *Mode al po'ndaa a bus chha na fe'raan,*
>
> *Akh ropai tsor anna dohas zenaan.*
>
> [These low-fare buses can't even take a proper turn,
>
> A rupee and four annas is all they earn.]

The crowd chuckled.

*As Gul's ballad unfolded over the next twenty minutes
or so, it addressed several issues, from the government's
inefficiencies to the plight of the poor to the foibles of
society, with pungent wit and straight-faced humour.*

*By the time Gul's performance ended, the audience was
howling with laughter. He closed his performance with
his signature refrain and was soon on his way to another
chowk in another village.*

> *Ladishah, ladishah dari kin peow,*
>
> *Pewnai pewnai haptan kheow.*
>
> [The ladishah fell off the window sloppily,
>
> Only to be bitten by a huge grizzly!]

Ladishahs, like Gul, were once a common sight in
Kashmir. In the era long before television and radio, these
itinerant singers brought news and entertainment to
country fairs and village squares. Although many of them
could barely read and write and learned their trade by
listening to older bards, they were the best oral historians
who addressed social, cultural and political issues with
satire and humour.

Dressed in pheran-pajama and with a chalk-white turban called the *dastaar* on their heads, their unique appearance was distinguishable even from a distance. To the jingle-jangle of the iron rings strung on their dhukri, they would sing parodies, humorous ballads and satirical songs that often took pot-shots at the well-heeled establishment. Sometimes they would criticize government actions or policies and at other times, expose the flaws and frailties of society.

Unlike other folk musicians, ladishahs wrote and composed their own songs and performed solo for about fifteen to twenty minutes. They seldom laughed themselves, leaving all the chuckles to the audience. Children followed these folk artists from one street to another and adults sang their songs at home—a testament to the popularity that ladishah once enjoyed in the Valley. Today, however, ladishahs can rarely be seen on the streets of Kashmir and are now confined to radio and television and even those appearances are infrequent.

THE THEATRE OF THE ABSURD

Whether it is *Hasyarnava Prahasanam*, a fourteenth-century political satire by Jagadesvara Bhattacharya, Premchand's *Shatranj Ke Khiladi,* or Shashi Tharoor's *The Great Indian Novel,* India has a rich history of satire that dates back to ancient times, especially in written traditions. Many Indian folk traditions also feature rib-cracking satires—particularly the folk traditions of Kashmir.

Ladishah is an important part of the traditional travelling folk theatre of Kashmir known as Bhand Pather.

The artists who performed in Bhand Pather were called Bhands and their theatrical performances were referred to as *pathers*. It is believed that during the medieval period, many court jesters from the Persian (present-day Iran) courts migrated to Kashmir and formed the Bhand community. At the foothills of the endless mountain ranges in Kashmir, there are over seventy villages where the majority of the Bhand population lives. These villages are locally called Bhand *gaams*.

Bharata's *Natyashastra*, a treatise on performing arts dated between the second century BCE and the fourth century CE, subtly references the satirical role of folk theatre in critiquing courtly plays. The *Nilamata Purana*, an ancient text from Kashmir, dating back to the sixth to eighth century CE and the *Rajatarangini*, a twelfth-century historical chronicle of Kashmir written by poet Kalhana, also mention *rangmandaps* (performances staged in courts and temple courtyards). However, these early references are often brief, leaving much of the folk theatre tradition undocumented.

The earliest references to the terms 'bhand' and 'pather' appear in the *shruks* (sayings) of Sheikh-ul-Alam, a fourteenth-century Kashmiri mystic. These performances typically took place in open meadows near Sufi shrines during the annual *urs* (death anniversaries) of Sufi saints. Large crowds gathered around the shrines to watch these performances, which were often based on Sufi legends. The performers were compensated in cash or kind by the spectators. The Bhands also performed mythological tales at Hindu temples, known locally as *bodh ghars*. During harvest time, they travelled from village to village, transforming courtyards or orchards into makeshift stages.

While their primary aim was to evoke laughter, these comedies often contained deeper messages hidden within the *phir kath* (roughly translated as twisted talk), a coded narrative that only those familiar with the local idiom could fully understand.

The Mughal invasion of 1586 CE, followed by the Afghan, Sikh and Dogra occupations, drastically altered the social fabric of Kashmir. These changes were reflected in the folk traditions of the Valley, including Bhand Pather. The performances began to mirror the people's growing sense of alienation and oppression under foreign rulers, by adopting a more satirical tone. The male performers, who dressed as women when the play demanded, moved from place to place and performed their skits based on socio-political issues to an enthusiastic native audience. Sir Walter Lawrence, in his book *The Valley of Kashmir* (1895), praised these travelling artists, calling them the 'remover of sorrows'.

Traditionally, Bhand Pather included elements of music, dance and buffoonery. The orchestra, known as Bhand Jashna or Bhand Chokk, included a dhol, a surnai—a wind instrument that has a strong, metallic sound that has an arresting effect in the open-air arena, a nagara (the Indian drum); and a pair of *thalij* (metal cymbals). Before the performance began, a nagara player went around the performance area in a circular motion, beating the drum to gather the audience.

The performers typically included a leader of the troupe called the *magun*—derived from the Sanskrit *mahaguni*, meaning a man of varied talents; the *mashkar* (jester) who carried out exaggerated actions to ridicule the exploitative actions of the authorities in the play; the *kuvirol,* who rebuked the mashkar for his politically incorrect behaviour and the *sutradhar*, who commented on the activities taking place. These characters could transform into different stock characters depending on the narrative.

The Bhand Pather performances were usually unscripted. They relied on the performers' improvisations and adapted to different public settings. Performers did not have a clearly defined acting area; they would often climb on to rooftops or trees and act according to their whims and fancies. One of the constant characters in these plays was that of a foreign ruler who carried a whip or bamboo stick symbolizing his tyranny. While the ruler spoke gibberish meant to sound like Persian or English, the other characters spoke Koshur, a language spoken by a majority of Kashmiris, creating misinterpretations and misunderstandings that led to humour. In the end, the mashkar usually fooled the ruler and taught him a lesson.

Since Bhand Pather performances took place in the open, the performers did not have stage curtains for costume changes or intervals. So, while the actors changed costumes and the performance paused, a traditional singer sang social and political chronicles of the time to the sounds of the dhukri. These situational ballads were comical in tone and tenor and were used as a tool to spread information and raise awareness.

At a time when people didn't have technology at their fingertips, these singers acted as a bridge of information, highlighting issues to people while also offering fun and entertainment. Over time, this custom of singing developed into an independent folk music tradition called ladishah.

THE BALLADS OF MALADIES

There is a marked difference of opinion among scholars regarding the definition and origin of ladishah. Some believe that it is a genre of poetry and singing while others maintain that denotes the narrator of the song. The exact origins are contested but many attribute its origin to the singing traditions of the roving poet-minstrels of Kashmir. (You can think of these singers as the medieval equivalent of today's singer and songwriters but without the big recording contracts—and instead of singing in concert halls, they performed on the streets.) The music of the poet-minstrels was monophonic, meaning there were no backup singers or duets. They typically used a string or percussion instrument such as a lute, fiddle or drums for accompaniment, with simple melodies and in the common language of the people.

One origin story says that ladishah is said to have got its name from one such wandering poet-minstrel from the village of Lari in the Pulwama district of south Kashmir during the late seventeenth century. Floods often ravaged the village as it was situated in a low-lying area near Kandizal, a vulnerable point on the course of Jhelum river. This poet-minstrel wrote satirical songs about the catastrophic consequences of these floods and sang them as he wandered from street to street. Since he was from the Shah community, a group of professional folk singers, he came to be known as Shah of Lari. The consonant sound 'R' is generally pronounced as

'D' in both Koshur and Urdu and therefore, over time, 'larishah' became ladishah and the genre got its name.

However, some historians argue that ladishah actually originates from the word 'ladi', which means rows or metrical lines of a verse. 'Shah' was added because this folk form developed during the rule of the Shah dynasty from the fourteenth to sixteenth centuries.

The tradition of ladishah flourished from the late sixteenth century until the early twentieth century when Kashmir was ruled by non-local rulers. In 1586 CE, after being defeated by the Kashmiri forces twice, the Mughal army entered the Valley and finally annexed it. After the Mughals, the Afghans established their rule in Kashmir in 1752 CE. The Sikhs fought many battles with the Afghans and finally annexed Kashmir in 1819. The British East India Company defeated the Sikh empire in the first Anglo-Sikh war in 1846 and 'sold' Kashmir for a lump sum of seventy-five lakh rupees to Gulab Singh, a commandant in the Dogra cavalry contingent of the Sikh army who had chosen to side with the British in the war.

The people of Kashmir suffered greatly in this prolonged period of systematic oppression by multiple rulers. The Afghans sent many Kashmiri people to Afghanistan as slaves and imposed exploitative taxes on the shawl weavers of the region. The Sikhs enacted anti-Muslim policies that angered the people of Kashmir, while the Dogra rulers imposed further taxes on them. Under the Dogra rulers, who owed their very existence to British patronage, the people of Kashmir were forced to fight in all of Britain's wars, including the two World Wars. Moreover, the eighteenth and nineteenth centuries saw a rise in natural disasters, including floods and earthquakes, in Kashmir.

In addition to being thought-provoking in subject matter, the songs of the ladishah were full of wry wit and painted vivid pictures of the ridiculous situations that common people often found themselves in during autocratic regimes. These narrative songs were written in short stanzas or couplets with end rhymes. They contained a refrain, or the first line was repeated at intervals. The language used in the songs was simple so the listeners could easily relate to the performance. As a reward, the ladishah would usually be given handfuls of rice by the audience at the end of the performance, which he collected in a bag hung around his shoulders.

In the songs of the ladishah, one can find illustrative details about colonial atrocities, administrative bungling, wealth disparities, religious superstitions, social evils and the destruction caused by natural calamities. Some significant pieces of ladishah include 'Angrez Qanoon' (the crisis of colonialism), *Sehlab Nama* (the chronicles of floods) and *Bunil Nama* (the chronicles of earthquakes). Hakeem Habibullah, Munawer Shah of Kulsoo and Lala Lakhman were some of the recognized masters of ladishah in the early twentieth century while Noor Mohammad Roshan and Mohammad Ali Kanwal were their contemporaries who carried forward the tradition of this folk ballad form.

A FOLK FORM VANISHES . . . AND THEN MAKES A FEEBLE RETURN

Before the 1950s, ladishah was one of the most popular folk ballad forms across Kashmir and its singers were a credible source of local and political news. However, the partition of India and Pakistan brought with it territorial conflicts between the two countries over Kashmir. Barely two months after India's independence, Pakistani soldiers invaded Jammu and Kashmir, leading to the first of the four wars that the two countries have fought since then. Over the next few decades, the reality of the Valley was riddled with turmoil and an uncertain political climate.

In this situation of heightened hostility and conflict, the importance given to folk traditions of Kashmir, such as ladishah, was completely lost. The advent of television also posed a serious threat to the indigenous folk traditions, but it was the eruption of militancy in Kashmir that delivered the final blow. In 1989, many militant groups began to emerge in the region that rejected ladishah for religious reasons. These groups, influenced by strict interpretations of Islam, considered street performances like ladishah, which integrated music and humour, as un-Islamic and a challenge to the conservative moral and social codes they sought to uphold. Only a handful of folk artists had continued to perform since the conflict began in the Valley in the 1950s but militancy put a complete stop to ladishah performances.

As political turmoil continued to sweep Kashmir, television became the main source of news and entertainment. Many of the senior ladishah performers passed away and the younger generations, unable to survive by pursuing their traditional vocation, took up alternate jobs such as weaving or carpentry.

In the last five years, however, a young generation of artists has been making concerted efforts to revive the age-old folk music. In urban Kashmir, for instance, ladishah is experiencing a revival in a new style. Some performers are exploring contemporary themes, such as media representation of the Valley, the shrinking space for dissent and arbitrary communication blackouts in their ladishah performances. Others are mixing modern aesthetics and sounds, such as electronica and rap, with the music inherited from their ancestors to connect with young people. Amplified by social networks and technological platforms that have helped broaden public access, the renewed wave of socially and politically conscious ladishah culture is slowly gaining traction in the Valley, largely in urban spaces.

AN ALTERNATE HISTORY

While stand-up comedy may be relatively new in India, its origins can be traced back to much older traditions. It inherits its iconoclasm, for instance, from the traditional folk satirists who spoke truth to power. Ladishah is one such community of folk artists who made people laugh, cry, rage and think.

Deeply rooted in the times, the ladishah tradition captured the voice of the common people in the absence of any other kind of documentation. It articulated public frustration during repressive regimes and addressed social issues when modern media was lacking. Interestingly, the performers sketched the darkness of the times in vibrant colours of satire and humour, transforming much of what was otherwise frightening into subjects of ridicule.

KASHMIR'S FIRST 'LADYSHAH'

One usual Sunday, the twenty-four-year-old Syed Areej Safvi watched a ladishah performance penned by Kashmiri journalist Rajesh Raina and performed by artist Rajinder Tickoo on TV. It spoke about highly political issues in a distinctly humorous way. On an impulse, Areej penned her first ladishah in her mother tongue, Koshur, about the abrupt abrogation of Article 370 of the Indian constitution which nullified the special status of Jammu and Kashmir and plunged the Valley into a state of lockdown, without internet connectivity and functioning telephone lines. Wearing a pheran, she recited the ladishah on her phone camera and posted the video on YouTube.

The video soon went viral, and Areej became the first woman in Kashmir to write and perform the ladishah. In her subsequent videos, Areej has touched upon issues such as COVID-19, power outage in Kashmir, the education system, and more. In a bid to revive ladishah, she conducts workshops in schools and introduces the folk form to young people.

The performers integrated art, language, performance and resistance in such a way that their songs told stories of common people, beyond hierarchies and presented a counter-history of the people of the Valley. Departing from the more stereotypical notions of a 'paradisical' Kashmir, the songs of the ladishah filled gaps in Kashmir's history and brought its many complexities to the fore.

Sadly, though, ladishah and many such expressions of dissent are no longer commonplace. As the young generation of ladishah folk artists continues to navigate the questions of survival, resistance and freedom to keep their unique brand of satirical singing alive, there is an urgent need to support them. If we don't, we risk losing not only a part of our collective heritage but also a crucial aspect of people's history.

LISTENING LIST:

Search words: Bhand Pather, Ladishah, Kashmiri Folk Theatre, Ladishah Gulzar Fighter, Ladishah Areej Syed

1. A clip of a ladishah performance featured in a documentary produced by the University of Kashmir.
   https://www.youtube.com/watch?v=29nANSbwBac

2. A clip of a Bhand Pather performance featured in a documentary produced by the University of Kashmir.
   https://www.youtube.com/watch?v=BEuElKujkJl

3. The renowned ladishah and Bhand performer Gulzar Bhat, also known as Gulzar Fighter, performs a ladishah.
   https://www.youtube.com/watch?v=YRVcVxHw7KQ

4. A modern take on the traditional ladishah by artist Umer Nazir.
   https://www.youtube.com/watch?v=R1i3UHrSAVw

5. A ladishah written and performed by Areej Syed, one of the few female ladishah artists from Kashmir.
   https://www.youtube.com/watch?v=XRAtsUW-Lzc

SONGS OF THE SUFIS

The Nizami Qawwali of Dilli

On Thursday nights, the shrine of the revered Chisti saint Hazrat Nizamuddin Auliya in south Delhi's Nizamuddin basti, one of the oldest settlements of the city, sees more visitors than usual. These special nights are believed to be occasions when Allah's rahmat (mercy) flows freely.

As one passes through the maze of lanes, with shops selling flowers, incense sticks, skull caps and attar, the low strain of music draws one closer to the shrine.

At the centre of the courtyard of the dargah, facing the brightly lit shrine of Hazrat Nizamuddin, a group of musicians gathers on this day every week. While the lead singer leads the group by singing a distinct form of devotional songs called the qawwali, the chorus brings in the rhythm by clapping and chanting the refrain as they progress from one hymn to the other. The effect of this call and repeat, combined with the beats of the claps, induces a spiritual trance.

It was in this same courtyard where the soulful notes of the qawwali first echoed towards the very end of the thirteenth century. According to legend, Hazrat

Nizamuddin Auliya's closest companion and devoted disciple Amir Khusrau set the following verse or *qaul* in Arabic, praising Hazrat Imam Ali, the cousin and son-in-law of Prophet Muhammad, to tune and created the first qawwali.

> *Man kunto maula,*
>
> *Fa hazaa aliyun maula.*
>
> [Whoever accepts me as a maula,
>
> Ali is his maula too.]

This 700-year-old tradition defines the musical landscape of the dargahs and *khanqahs* (multi-purpose complexes), where Sufi saints lived and met their devotees across India. It is carried forward by a group of musicians united by their common descent from a Sufi *silsila* (order). The musicians who trace back their musical lineage to the Nizamuddin dargah are collectively known as the Nizamis and their rich culture of qawwali is tied intrinsically to the legends of Nizamuddin and Khusrau.

SUFISM IN INDIA

In the seventh and eighth centuries CE, Sufism (*tasawwuf* in Arabic), a mystical tradition emphasizing a personal experience of god through love and harmony, began to blossom within Islam. Over time, many itinerant saints chose the path of Sufism and dedicated their lives to introducing the philosophy to the local populace in an organized way. These saints were considered the spiritual messengers of god and some of them emerged as masters of Sufi philosophy, particularly in Egypt, Syria, Iraq, Turkey and Arabia. In its early years, the tradition spread in small circles led by Sufi leaders or guides. As the number of practitioners grew, mystical orders or groups formed around the teachings of these leaders, leading to the written documentation of Sufi tenets.

Many *khwajas* (Sufi saints) arrived in India during the eleventh and twelfth centuries. One of them was Khwaja Moinuddin Chisti, born in Sijistan (present-day Sistan in Iran) in 1141 CE as Moinuddin Hasan. He abandoned all worldly comforts early in life to practice austerities under the Sufi saint Sheikh Usman Harawani of the Chisti tariqa (order), founded in 930 CE in Chist near Herat, Afghanistan.

THE PATRON SAINT OF THE POOR

Khwaja Moinuddin Chisti was lovingly called Garib Nawaz or 'patron of the poor'. Thousands were fed at his dargah daily. His dargah in Ajmer has two huge *deghs* (cauldrons) donated by Mughal emperors, Akbar and Jahangir, in which food is cooked and distributed among the poor. The pot presented by Akbar, called the Badi Degh, holds 4,800 kg of food and the one by Jahangir, called the Choti Degh, holds 2,400 kg of food. Many grateful devotees whose prayers have been fulfilled contribute to it daily.

When Moinuddin Chisti was about fifty-one, Sheikh Usman gave him a *khirqah* (patched cloak of successorship) and made him his spiritual successor. Moinuddin went on a pilgrimage to Mecca and Medina and while praying in a mosque in Medina, he is believed to have heard the Prophet instructing him to go to the city of Ajmer in Hindustan. Though Moinuddin had no idea where Ajmer was, he travelled to Lahore via Baghdad and Herat and, from there, reached Delhi and then Ajmer in 1192 CE. He settled in Ajmer and introduced the Chisti order in India. Soon, his teachings drew people from far and wide, who became his disciples.

As a part of the spiritual practice of dhikr (remembering god by repeating his name), Khwaja Moinuddin Chisti and his disciples participated in a traditional musical gathering called *mehfil-e-sama* that had been popular among the Sufis in central Iraq, Egypt and Morocco. A gathering for spiritual listening, mehfil-e-sama involved the coming together of Sufis in a shrine after dusk to recite verses that invoke the glory of god. These performances often included reciting poetry, singing, wearing symbolic attire and other rituals. It is believed that decades later, this practice was expanded and codified as a musical form called qawwali by a mystic poet and musician who was a disciple of the twelfth-century Sufi saint Nizamuddin.

THE AURA OF HAZRAT NIZAMUDDIN AULIYA

Delhi is known to be the spiritual capital of Indian Sufism and is historically revered among Sufis as *bais khwajaaon ki chaukhat,* the city of the twenty-two most prominent saints. However, Nizamuddin and his favourite disciple Khusrau hold a special significance.

Khwaja Moinuddin Chisti appointed his disciple Khwaja Qutbuddin Bakhtiyar Kaki as his spiritual successor. After Kaki's demise, his disciple Baba Fariduddin Ganjshakar, better known as Baba Farid, carried forward the tradition. Following Baba Farid's death, his disciple, Nizamuddin, became the fourth sheikh or spiritual successor of the Chisti order in India.

Born in 1238 CE in Badaun, Uttar Pradesh, Nizamuddin lost his father at the age of five which prompted the family's move to Delhi. Even as a teenager, he distinguished himself as a scholar and great debater. He initially considered becoming a qazi (cleric) but later changed his mind and decided to pursue his quest for divine knowledge. At the age of twenty, he travelled to Ajodhan, a village in Pakpattan (present-day Pakistan), to meet Baba Farid, whose fame had spread through the subcontinent. When he met the ninety-year-old Sufi saint at the Jama Khana (the convent), Baba Farid welcomed Nizamuddin with these words: 'O the fire of separation of Thee has burnt many hearts. The storm of desire to meet Thee has ravaged many lives.' On Nizamuddin's third visit, Baba Farid declared him his successor by offering him the special turban which he had received from his *pir-o-murshid* (spiritual guide). Nizamuddin lived in the company of his spiritual guide for seven months before Baba Farid passed away.

Nizamuddin travelled the length and breadth of the country to spread Sufi teachings and finally settled in a quiet neighbourhood of Ghiyaspur (present-day Nizamuddin Basti) in the imperial city of Delhi. He built a khanqah there—a place where people from all walks of life were fed and spiritual teachings were imparted. Soon, it attracted people from different faiths, young and old, illiterate and educated, rich and poor and Nizamuddin came to be known as *Mehboob-e-Ilahi* (the beloved of god).

HAZRAT NIZAMUDDIN'S FAVOURITE DISCIPLE

When Nizamuddin was about twenty-three,
eight-year-old Khusrau (born Abul Hasan Yameenuddin),
accompanied his father, Amir Saifuddin, to his khanqah.
A nobleman from Balkh (present-day Afghanistan), Amir
Saifuddin had fled from the Mongols to India and joined
the court of Sultan Iltutmish of the Mamluk dynasty, which
ruled the Delhi sultanate from 1206 CE to 1290 CE. When
his father went inside the khanqah, the young Abul, who
had remarkable poetic abilities even as a child, remained at
the door. He wanted to test the saint out, so he composed
a poem, asking the saint whether he should cross the
threshold to enter the khanqah or return home.

> *Tu an Shah-e-ke bar aiwan-e-qasrat,*
>
> *Kabutar gar nashinad baz garded.*
>
> *Gharib-e mustanande baradar amad,*
>
> *Be ayat andar un ya baz gardad.*
>
> [You are a mighty king, at the gates of whose palace
>
> Even a pigeon becomes a hawk.
>
> A rank outsider has come to your doorstep,
>
> Please let him know whether he should come inside or leave.]

It is said that Nizamuddin asked one of his attendants to
go to the gate at once and recite the following lines to the
boy outside:

> *Biya yet andarun marde haqiqat,*
>
> *Kibama yak nafas hamraz gardad,*
>
> *Agar ablah buwad an mard nadan,*
>
> *Azan rahe ki amad baz gardad.*

[He who knows the truth may come inside,

So that we can exchange divine secrets between us.

If he is ignorant, then he must return

To the same path he has come from.]

Hearing this, Abul ran inside to meet Nizamuddin. Ecstatic beyond measure, he is believed to have sung: '*Aaj rung hai, hey maa rung hai ri. Moray mehboob kay ghar rung hai ri, mohay pir paayo Nizamuddin Auliya.*' (What a glow everywhere I see. Oh mother, what a glow! I have found my master. Yes, I have found Nizamuddin Auliya.) And, with this, Khusrau's search for a Sufi master ended.

Khusrau's career began at the age of twenty as a poet in the court of Ghiyas-ud-din Balban, a Mamluk sultan. Khusrau served seven different rulers from 1272 CE to 1325 CE. While he was an *amir* (noble) in these royal courts, he sought spiritual solace at the khanqah of his pir (spiritual guide) Nizamuddin.

Khusrau wrote in both Persian, the official and literary language that was used by the *ashrafs* (elites) in the royal courts of the Delhi sultanate and Hindawi (a mixture of Khari Boli, Braj Bhasha and Awadhi dialects) which was the language of the *ajlafs* (common people). The same Hindawi later developed into two languages—Hindi and Urdu.

Khusrau was also a great musician and composer, an innovative inventor and a venerated linguist, scholar and historian. He is credited with enriching Hindustani classical music by introducing Persian and Arabic elements and composing many new ragas. *Khayal* and *tarana*, two popular forms of Hindustani classical music, are believed to have been pioneered by him. Khayal is a genre of Indian classical music that enables imaginative interpretations of ragas. Tarana, on the other hand, incorporates specific words and syllables arranged in rhythmic patterns, adding a distinctive dimension to classical performances.

MELODIES OF THE PAST

Among the many priceless treasures housed in the National Museum, New Delhi, there is an eighteenth-century Deccani miniature painting of Hazrat Nizamuddin Auliya. Dressed in an olive-green robe—the colour associated with heavenly bliss in Sufism—and with a halo around his head, he is seated in a courtyard overlooking a mango tree, listening to music played by Amir Khusrau. Holding a musical instrument in his right hand, Khusrau appears to be singing songs of the divine as beautiful red flowers sway in the background.

At first glance, the painting might seem straightforward. However, upon closer inspection, it reveals layers of history, unlocking stories about the origins of Indo-Muslim musical traditions. What is the song that Amir Khusrau is singing? Could it be a qawwali? What is the instrument that he is holding?

Khusrau made significant contributions to the development of the then-existing sitar, the grand Indian lute and invented the Indian tabla. He is also remembered as a founder of the Ganga-Jamuni Tehzeeb, or the Indian culture which is a synthesis of Muslim and Hindu elements. Khusrau's impact on India's cultural landscape is so profound that even after centuries, not a day goes by in the life of ordinary Indians without encountering one of his linguistic and musical innovations—often without realizing their origins. But there is one more thing that Khusrau created—qawwali.

QAWWAL BACHCHE

While musical traditions typically evolve over centuries with contributions from many different people, some musicians give a definite form to existing practices. Amir Khusrau was one such musician gave a definitive structure to was the mehfil-e-sama popular among the Sufis.

Legend has it that Nizamuddin was once upset and Khusrau, determined to bring a smile to his pir's face, turned to music. He selected some qauls praising god and sought to set them to music. However, when he tried to use the classical musical forms of that time, he found them too constrained by strict rules. So, he tried to liberate the traditional Hindustani music from its rigid grammar by blending it with musical elements from Turkey and Persia. This fusion gave birth to the unique musical expression we now know as qawwali.

Khusrau selected twelve gifted disciples and trained them in the new form. He gave lessons to them on the musical basis of this form as well as in the *adab-o-adaab* (codes of conduct) pertinent to its performance. These students, known as the Qawwal Bachche, performed for Nizamuddin who was thrilled with their performance.

The tradition—unbroken for over 700 years—has been passed down orally to those associated with the twelve original disciples of Khusrau, either genealogically or musically and came to be known as the Nizami qawwali. The word 'Nizami' literally means the one following the Nizam or the creator, but it also means the followers of Nizamuddin. The poetic repertoire of the Nizami qawwals consists of a variety of texts reflecting themes of divine love, spiritual longing and the teachings of Sufi saints, all taught to them by their teachers. The same version of the song, including lyrics, tunes and tonality, is used by all descendants.

Traditionally, a qawwali performance has eleven male musicians, usually dressed in black or white. There are three prerequisites for creating *sama* (spiritual atmosphere) in which qawwali must be sung. The first is *zaman*, meaning time—there is a designated time for offering qawwalis at the shrines to avoid clashing with the daily *namaaz* (prayers). The second is *makaan*, which means the place where the qawwali is sung must be sacred. And lastly, *ikhwan*, which means companions. The careful attention given to atmosphere and audience in the Sufi tradition distinguished the performance of qawwali from an ordinary musical assembly.

One of the most distinct features of the qawwali performance is the clapping as the qawwals believe that the body itself is a rhythmic instrument. Initially, qawwali involved only vocals and clapping. But, over time, the use of musical instruments such as the harmonium, tabla, *pakhavaj* and *esraj* became more common.

The qawwali performance follows a definite progression—beginning with a slow rhythm and ending with powerful, high notes and a rapidly increasing tempo. It usually starts with an instrumental prelude, followed by an introductory verse sung without any rhythmic accompaniment, the main song and a closing song. The chorus often dwells on a single phrase, repeating various words and emphasizing certain syllables to ensure the audience fully internalizes the various layers of meaning of the verse.

Over the years, qawwali began to be performed outside of the dargahs and khanqahs as well. Soon, it gained popularity through various media, including radio, television, movies, digital platforms and concerts, enabling a wider audience to experience the magic of qawwali.

But when, why and how did qawwali move out of the shrines to become a part of concerts and movies? Although the specifics are unclear, it was likely an evolutionary process that began in the early years of the twentieth century.

QAWWALI DOWN THE AGES

Any musical tradition, with each succeeding generation, adapts, evolves and reshapes itself, harkening back to its roots while gently metamorphosing into something subtly new. For centuries, there were no changes in how and where qawwali was performed. This stability lasted for about 600 years, with qawwali largely remaining within shrine settings as a spiritual practice. However, by the turn of the nineteenth century, qawwalis began to transform. If you have seen singers wearing slanted fur caps, kerchiefs around their necks and clapping in a certain style in Hindi movies, then you are already familiar with the transformation that qawwali underwent to capture the popular imagination.

The introduction of recording technology in the early twentieth century enabled the reproduction and mass distribution of sound recordings. Soon after, the advent of radio transformed popular culture. The qawwals were among the first Indian artists to be recorded by the British Gramophone Company in Calcutta in 1902 as urban professional performers. These qawwalis were in simple Urdu, unlike the religious qawwali which used literary Urdu.

Although not based on classical Sufi poems, the recorded qawwalis echoed traditional themes, making them accessible to listeners of all backgrounds. By the late 1930s, several recording companies were in operation and qawwali gained enduring fame with numerous records that people could now listen to at home.

Shortly afterward, qawwali began to be used in Parsi theatre, a theatrical tradition considered the predecessor of popular Hindi cinema or 'Bollywood'. In the black-and-white film era of the 1940s and 1950s, when Urdu was used for writing songs, qawwali made its way to the big screen. Over the next couple of decades, it evolved to include not just devotion, but romance, comedy and even social commentary. Moreover, qawwalis in movies also started to feature female singers. In the 1970s and 1980s, known as the golden decade of qawwali, many qawwali sequences featured in movies as a narrative device used to advance the plot. Hindi movies also helped popularize a form of secular qawwali known as *muqable ki qawwali,* where two groups of qawwali singers competed to outdo each other in improvised verses.

In the 1990s, singers such as Nusrat Fateh Ali Khan and the Sabri Brothers took qawwali to the global stage, while composers like A.R. Rahman modernized it with electronic tunes. Today, qawwali continues to flourish through the talents of artists like the Nooran sisters and Rahat Fateh Ali Khan.

The evolution of qawwali in the last hundred years is a testament to its enduring appeal and impact. While adapting to contemporary contexts in concert halls and popular cinema, qawwali retains its historical roots as a unique form of devotional music. Drawing from the original Sufi ritual of mehfil-e-sama, the local qawwals at dargahs across India continue to stir emotions and evoke a sense of community defined not just by faith but by poetry and pluralism.

So, if you ever get a chance to visit the dargah of Nizamuddin in Delhi and listen to the Nizami qawwali, do so by all means. It would be a great opportunity to witness a centuries-old tradition—and have a musically good time!

LISTENING LIST:

Search words: Qawwali, Qawwal Bachche, Nizami Qawwali, Dilli Gharana, Nizami Bandhu, Nusrat Fateh Ali Khan, Fareed Fayaz, Abu Muhammad

1. Ustad Meraj Ahmed Nizami's beautiful rendition of 'Man Kunto Maula'.
   https://www.youtube.com/watch?v=GbKvwLTUzcU

2. Nusrat Fateh Ali Khan's rendition of 'Aaj Rang Hai' showcasing his unparalleled qawwali artistry.
   https://www.youtube.com/watch?v=1posCYyyxeg

3. The qawwali 'Chhap Tilak Sab Chheeni Re' by Nizami Bandhu, a timeless rendition of Ameer Khusro's classic.
   https://www.youtube.com/watch?v=M8JrmgdOVAU

4. The qawwali 'Kun Faaya Kun' from the movie *Rockstar*, written by Irshad Kamil, composed by A.R. Rahman and sung by Javed Ali, Mohit Chauhan and A.R. Rahman.
   https://www.youtube.com/watch?v=olQ4JFaObHQ

5. The soulful qawwali 'Aadam' by Fareed Ayaz and Abu Muhammad from Coke Studio Pakistan, originally composed by Amir Khusrau.
   https://www.youtube.com/watch?v=BQ74szweuZw

SONGS OF THE PANDAVAS

The Pandavani Folk Music of Chhattisgarh

Dressed in a bright red sari, the fabric draped just above her ankles, Teejan Bai strides on to the stage, her festooned tambura—a long-necked three-stringed lute—held aloft like a menacing mace. She closes her eyes, takes a deep breath and plucks the stiff strings of her tambura producing a sound that resonates with an otherworldly note. A moment later, she invokes Lord Krishna in her booming voice: 'Bol do Vrindavan Bihari lal ki jai . . . More sana nana nana . . .'

Then, she begins a ballad from the epic Mahabharata that transports the audience to Hastinapur, or Hasna-Nagri as she calls it.

Arey Pandav charit suno, sabha mein hovat baani,

Dhritarashtra ke darbar mein, bhari sabha kahani.

[Listen to the tale of the Pandavas, what happens in the court,

In Dhritarashtra's assembly, a story unfolds.]

Teejan Bai thunders across the stage, bringing to life legendary characters—the mighty Bheema, the feisty Draupadi, the sly Shakuni and the mystical Krishna. She becomes one with the story she is narrating—plots

unravel, scenes unfold and courtrooms, inner chambers and battlefields appear out of thin air.

The main accompanist, the ragi, *in her* mandali *(singing party) of musicians, becomes the symbolic audience and interjects her narration with loud retorts such as* 'hun, hun, haho!' *(yes, yes, yes),* 'aichcha, hau!' *(really!),* 'kaabar?' *(why?) to spice up the performance.*

When the performance ends, the audience marvels at the magical journey that transported them to a different time and space and swept their senses away.

The folk singing tradition from Chhattisgarh for which Teejan Bai is renowned is called Pandavani, or the songs of the Pandavas, the legendary brothers in the Mahabharata. It is said that everything that can happen in life has happened in the Mahabharata. Composed over a thousand years ago, scholars pin the Mahabharata's oral origins to around 400 BCE, when different versions of its constituent stories were sung by bards and priests. It was only in 400 CE that these stories came to be compiled into a written text in Sanskrit, with over 100,000 verses across eighteen *parvas* (sections).

For centuries, the Mahabharata has been read, heard, seen, told, sung and performed in temples and fairs, during festivals and social occasions, in different languages, contexts and styles, by dancers, singers, writers, poets, painters and minstrels across the Indian subcontinent. Each region adds its own local references, linguistic expressions and contextual subtexts, hence, there exist many different versions of the same stories.

THE GONDI PANDAVANI

The origins of Pandavani can be traced to the oral lore of the Gonds, one of the largest ethnic-linguistic communities of central India, known as Gondwana around the fourteenth century. The stories of the Mahabharata were sung and recited widely by the storyteller-singer sub-tribes of the Gond community, such as the Pardhans, Dewars and Satnamis. Traditionally, to the sounds of the *kingri*, a bowed string instrument, these itinerant performers would visit their patron lords and ladies after every harvest season and sing from memory the patron's genealogies and local versions of the epics of Ramayana and Mahabharata in the Chhattisgarhi language, called the Ramayani and the Pandavani respectively. In return, they would be offered gifts of grains, clothes and sometimes even cattle and gold.

The Gond oral traditions are closely tied to the Mahabharata, particularly through the association of the Pandavas to the Gond region. Episodes from the Mahabharata are recounted with a blend of storytelling, music and drama, often focusing on the *agyatvasa*—the twelve-year exile of the Pandavas in the forests of the Gondwana region. In these narratives, the events of the Mahabharata are reinterpreted in the socio-cultural setting of the region, with characters designed according to the local imagination and several Gond myths and legends interwoven into the stories. Many scholars believe that these folk ballads existed even before the Mahabharata assumed a written form.

Bheema, often portrayed as a secondary character in televised versions of the Mahabharata, is featured as a central figure in these songs. Known by various names such as Bhima, Bhimma, Bhimsen, Bimai and Bhimul, he is associated with several popular myths in the region. One such myth links him to a musical instrument called the *mandar*, which is believed to bring rain when played. Another popular tale is the 'Byah Katha', the story of the marriage of each of the Pandavas, with Bheema as the protagonist. These performances sometimes also focus on minor stories from the Mahabharata, such as that of Ghatotkacha, Bheema's son.

Gradually, these performances attracted the patronage of the wealthy landowners of the region and over time this unique practice transformed into a performative genre.

THE CULT OF BHEEMA

In the folklore of central India, Bheema is worshipped as an Adivasi hero. The Gonds, for instance, believe that they learned the technique of farming from him and that he is responsible for bringing rain. Villages across Chhattisgarh have many sacred shrines, ponds, hills and waterfalls named after Bheema.

Every year during monsoons, the Gonds celebrate Bheema jatra, the marriage of Bheema with Bheemi. Elaborate murals are drawn on the walls of temporary shrines outside the villages. A pole representing Bheema is installed near each shrine, covered with cow dung to trap Bheema's spirit inside the pole, who will then impel Lord Indra to release rain to wash off the dung and set him free.

THE MERRY ADVENTURES OF
THE MAMA-BHANJA

Until the late nineteenth century, Pandavani was sung by itinerant singers whose names we do not know, for their patrons and remained confined within village precincts. But then came a performer duo, popularly known as Mama-Bhanja, who are the earliest performers of whom there are records. They introduced Pandavani as a distinct performative narrative form, to a wider audience.

Originally from the village of Ravana-Jheepan, Narayan Lal Verma and his young nephew, Bhuvan Lal Verma, sang stories of the Pandavas in their inimitable styles at the village *haats* and *chaurahas* in the Raipur-Bilaspur region. Standing in the light of a *mashaal* (flaming torch), they began their tales with *'Ram, ram bhaiyya'* and sang them to the music of the khartal, khanjari and chikara. Without a microphone or stage, Narayan Lal Verma narrated stories in a guttural voice with unmatched verve and mesmerized the audience. As he recounted the episodes from the Mahabharata, his young nephew provided humorous repartee that the audience enjoyed very much. Bhuvan Lal would interject questions or predict the plot twists and would alter his uncle's storytelling to enhance the audience's experience— emphasizing comedy or pathos, or sharing titbits about their favourite minor characters.

The entire village gathered to listen to the stories of Mama-Bhanja, who spun these tales late into the night. Narayan Lal would vividly recreate scenes with his words and gestures, varying his tone and pitch to keep the audience enthralled. These seemingly endless tales were picked up the next night from the point where Mama-Bhanja had left off.

THE FIRST WOMAN SINGER OF THE PANDAVANI

Around the time the Mama-Bhanja duo performed, a woman singer named Sukhiya Bai also performed Pandavani. She is regarded as the first female Pandavani singer. Originally from Mungi village near Raipur, Sukhiya Bai would perform in the guise of a man, as Pandavani was considered a male tradition. Dressed in a kurta and dhoti, she took the stage to sing of the struggles and triumphs of the Pandavas.

The Mama-Bhanja duo wove such magic with their performances that the audience was spellbound night after night. Their performances became a phenomenon in the region, but there was a downside. Whenever the Mama-Bhanja duo performed, a notorious gang of thieves would raid the villagers' homes. Unable to manage the law-and-order situation, the police arrested the duo and put them in jail. Even in prison, the duo continued to sing the Pandavani for the inmates. The police eventually released them but imposed a condition—they could no longer perform Pandavani through the night—an embargo that is still observed today.

CULTURAL MEMORY VERSUS THE WRITTEN WORD

For the longest time, the songs of Pandavani narrated adventures of the Pandavas in disjointed bits and pieces. Though part of the great epic of the Mahabharata, these songs had a life outside of the original text and were transmitted orally within the communities. In the 1940s, a weaver-singer, Jhaduram Dewangan, transformed the Pandavani narrative by basing it on the actual text, shifting the tradition from its oral roots.

From the Dewangan community of weavers in Chhattisgarh, Jhaduram was commissioned to weave a Kosa silk saree. When Jhaduram went to deliver it, the buyer did not have the money to pay for it. Instead, he gave Jhaduram a copy of the Mahabharata, retold in the Awadhi language by the sixteenth-century poet Sabal Singh Chauhan. Since the written version of the epic was typically accessible only to the upper castes who had the money to buy books, this was Jhaduram's first exposure to the text and he was completely mesmerized. As his fingers moved to the rhythms of his handloom, the young weaver memorized the entire text and began singing it to the local tunes.

One day, Jhaduram heard a famous Pandavani singer, Itvari Sahu, sing an episode from the Mahabharata. He noticed several deviations from the text he had read, including numerous additions from the singer's imagination. When Jhaduram pointed these out, Itvari Sahu challenged him to a musical contest. Jhaduram Dewangan won the vocal duel.

This episode led to a shift in the way the Pandavani folk tradition was perceived. When Jhaduram challenged the textual deviations, a stigma came to be attached to the 'inauthentic' and 'imaginary' ways of singing Pandavani. Gradually, the songs that had evolved out of the region and carried local colour and flavour were revised. The local elements were combed out from the lyrics of these songs and replaced with the Mahabharata of Sabal Singh Chauhan which was written in a *doha-chaupai* (couplet-and-quatrain) style.

As the text-based Pandavani started gaining ground, the practice of singing indigenous lore was devalued and began to be seen as a corruption of the classical text. Its performers were barred from performing in public. This led to polarization among the performers, with some like Jhaduram, wishing to enhance the stature of Pandavani by lending it a sacred aura, while others insisting that it is a part of indigenous creativity that has existed in the vibrant folkloric traditions of the region since time immemorial and must remain as such.

TWO MAJOR SCHOOLS OF PANDAVANI

After Independence in 1947, there was a reappraisal of folk traditions, with an emphasis on promoting the diversity of age-old cultural practices. Regional folk traditions were celebrated in festivals organized by the government across India. Cultural institutions, such as the Sangeet Natak Akademi, the Lalit Kala Akademi and the National School of Drama, were established to preserve and promote indigenous art forms. The rise of radio and TV also created a demand for professional artists, leading many to reclaim traditional art forms.

This, in turn, led to the evolution of two distinct styles in which Pandavani was performed—the *vedamati shaili* (style based on the scriptures) and the *kapalik shaili* (a free-flowing style with scope for improvisation). By the 1960s, the distinction between these two styles was quite clear.

Gradually, Pandavani expanded in scope to include different styles of rendition. Performed earlier by a lead performer and his ragi with one or two instruments, performers began to form mandalis. Along with changes in what was recited, how it was recited also evolved. The vedamati style consisted of pure ballad singing, mostly by a main performer who sang couplets from the text in a seated position, focusing on a traditional and restrained delivery. In contrast, the kapalik style included *gammat* (improvisation) as a distinctive trait, with added theatrics to embellish the tales. These two styles correspond to the different content and performance approaches within Pandavani, making them suited to specific types of storytelling.

From the oral lore recited by the Gond Pardhans mainly during important social occasions, Pandavani came to be performed at festivals and events where the audiences flocked to hear the story for its own sake.

Pandavani, especially in the kapalik style, was performed exclusively by male performers till the 1970s as women were forbidden to perform in public. Teejan Bai gave Pandavani not just a new voice but also a new context. A one-woman theatre, she redefined the tradition both in form and content and her story is almost as dramatic as the epic she has been recounting for the last six decades.

TEEJAN BAI: THE POWERHOUSE OF PANDAVANI

Teejan Bai was born on 24 April 1956 in a small village called Ganiyari, north of Bhilai in Chhattisgarh. Her parents, Sukhwati and Chunuk Lala Pardhi, belonged to the Pardhi tribe and made a living by making and selling brooms and straw mats. The family lived in a roadside shack and could barely manage a daily meal.

When Teejan was a child, she heard her maternal grandfather, Brijlal Pardhi, a Pandavani artist, recite the Mahabharata and felt a *jhunjhuni* (strange sensation) that she could not shake off. For an entire week, she hid and listened to her grandfather's stories. She wanted to learn to recite them and make them her own.

One day, Brijlal Pardhi caught her listening to the stories and offered to teach her. But Teejan was scared to tell her mother. So, she came up with an idea—Teejan would look after her younger siblings during the day and then sneak out in the evenings to learn Pandavani from her grandfather! With a tambura held aloft in one hand, she was practising a story from the Mahabharata one evening when her mother saw her and slapped her hard. She was locked up and not given any food.

At the age of twelve, Teejan was married off. But soon, her marriage ended abruptly. Much against the wishes of her family, Brijlal Pardhi decided to continue teaching her the art of Pandavani. For one whole month, Teejan listened to her grandfather sing the 'Adiparv', the first of the eighteen parvas in the Mahabharata. She learned the entire episode, not fully understanding the words but memorizing them through repetition. She then chose the kapalik style to perform it. Since this style was more theatrical and involved dance and enactment, her family was furious but Teejan was not one to be deterred.

One night, Teejan was beaten badly and thrown out of the house. She ran away to the nearby village of Chandrakhuri. Making a living by weaving brooms, she was discovered by a man from the village who heard her sing and asked her to perform Pandavani for fifteen days. Her determination was finally rewarded. She gave her first performance on a makeshift stage for a sum of ten rupees and a sackful of rice. She sold the rice, went back to her village and used the money to build the roof of her house.

Teejan decided to train informally under the ragi Umed Singh Deshmukh. Gradually, she started employing a range of stylistic tools in her performance, including semi-musical narration, songs, acting and offering a critique of the happenings in the narrative. She took stories from Sabal Singh Chauhan's version of the Mahabharata—though not in the same metrical pattern—and recreated, improvised and contemporized them extensively. She also focused on the sensitive gender equations in the epic through her narrations.

By the early 1980s, Teejan Bai had become popular in the region. Indian playwright Habib Tanvir, considered one of the pioneers of Indian theatre for introducing folk and tribal elements into his plays, noticed her talent and invited her and some other Pandavani artists to perform for the then prime minister of India, Indira Gandhi. Invitations started pouring in from all over the world after that, and by 1986, Teejan Bai had performed in over 2,000 shows globally.

For close to six decades now, Teejan Bai has single-handedly taken Pandavani to the farthest corners of the world and has thus saved it from fading into oblivion. For her contribution to the folk culture, she has received several prestigious awards, including the Padma Shri in 1988 and the Padma Bhushan in 2003.

Today, many artists such as Meena Sahu, Prabha Yadav, Ritu Verma, Kumari Nishad, Chameli Nishad, Indira Jhangde, Amrita Sahu, Pratima Barle, Kunti Gandharva, Jana Bai Satnami and Purnima Sahu are advancing both the vedamati and kapalik traditions of Pandavani, keeping the vibrancy of central India's folk traditions alive in their songs.

TRADITIONS WITH VARIATIONS

The great folklorist A.K. Ramanujan observed that the Mahabharata is not merely a text but a living tradition, manifesting uniquely across various communities in India through songs, sayings, performances and festivals. Here are a few of these traditions:

Thoda (Himachal Pradesh): Originating in Kullu, *thoda* is a traditional archery form combined with music and dance, believed to be a martial art practised by the Pandavas and Kauravas.

Vyahgowa Ojapali (Assam): This ancient art form involves *ojas* (chorus leaders) and *palis* (assistants) who narrate the Bhagavata, Mahabharata and Harivamsa through song and dance.

Pandonritya (Uttarakhand): In Garhwal, *Pandonritya* is a ritualistic performance that reenacts Mahabharata stories through singing, dancing and recitation.

Bhilon Nu Bharat (Gujarat): This oral version of the Mahabharata preserved by the Bhil tribe reflects their unique perspective, with stories recited or sung during festivals.

Chitrakathi (Maharashtra): *Chitrakathi*, once popular in Maharashtra and Karnataka, uses wooden puppets or paintings to tell stories from the Ramayana and Mahabharata.

Pandun Ka Kada (Rajasthan): Known as the Pandavas' couplets, this tradition involves the Jogi and Meo communities of Mewat reciting and singing dohas that elaborate on the themes of the Mahabharata.

Theerukoothu (Tamil Nadu): A folk theatre form integrating drama, song and dance, *theerukoothu* dramatizes Tamil versions of the Mahabharata, with Draupadi as the central deity worshipped in the performance.

THE MANY MAHABHARATAS

The oral storytelling traditions across the world are as old as language itself. In India, orality still dominates as a significant portion of the population lives in remote, inaccessible areas and many of the languages spoken do not have a written form. One of the most widely known and most loved epics of our nation, the Mahabharata, for instance, is known to have existed and passed down orally for over a millennium before it was written down. And even after it was transcribed, the epic continued to be recited more often than read.

This enduring oral tradition is evident in the Mahabharata's ability to inspire countless retellings and interpretations across diverse contexts. The epic's survival is evidence of its flexibility and its capacity to resonate deeply with different communities. Despite the mainstream Mahabharata written in Sanskrit dominating popular imagination, each Adivasi community—whether the Gonds, Bhils, Mundas, Santhals, Sauras, Korkus, or Rabhas—has developed its own unique Mahabharata tradition, with distinct characters and events. These traditions are enriched with visual and performative narratives that are deeply interwoven with the community's way of life. While retaining the thematic core, these communities have infused their Mahabharatas with local culture, customs, language and geographical details.

These diverse Mahabharata folk and tribal traditions, including Pandavani, challenge the notion of a single, dominant narrative and ignite both individual and collective imaginations. And the glory of these traditions lives on in the stories told, songs sung, plays performed, images inscribed and genealogies committed to memory—rather than in the pages of a book.

LISTENING LIST:

Search words: Pandavani, Chhattisgarh Folk Music, Vedamati Pandavani, Kapalik Pandavani, Chetan Devangan, Teejan Bai, Usha Barle, Ritu Verma, Prabha Yadav, Mahabharata Folk Performance

1. A Pandavani performance by Teejan Bai at a culture festival held at the Indira Gandhi National Centre for Arts (IGNCA). https://www.youtube.com/watch?v=j-aCj6-WkTo

2. Chetan Dewangan, chief disciple of renowned Pandavani singer Jhaduram Devangan, performs Pandavani in the vedamati style. https://www.youtube.com/watch?v=EOEign-H7Y4

3. Prabha Yadav, a distinguished vedamati style performer, presents the 'Musal' and 'Swargarohan' parva of the Mahabharata. https://www.youtube.com/watch?v=41ouCK-5uu8

4. A kapalik rendition of the Pandavani by Ritu Verma, a contemporary artist who's been performing since the age of six.
https://www.youtube.com/watch?v=kqnnTxN39SI

5. Padma Shri awardee Usha Barle performs Pandavani in the kapalik style.
https://www.youtube.com/watch?v=-ehjfKfWelk

SONGS OF THE LOOM

The Kabir Vaani of the Vankar Community of Kutch

In the open courtyard of a house in Bhujodi, a village located about fourteen kilometres from Bhuj in the Kutch district of Gujarat, the male weavers of the family bend over their wooden looms, weaving the delicately hued dhablas (shawls). Nearby, amidst rows of dyed fabrics that hang from ropes strung across the courtyard, the women of the family prepare the yarn on their spinning wheels while the children wind colourful threads around bobbins.

The clickety-clack of the looms reverberates through the still afternoon air as the weavers move their nimble fingers through bundles of yarn to design the most intricate patterns. To keep pace with the rhythmic sound of the loom, they break into a song written by the fifteenth-century weaver-poet Kabir. This song uses the metaphor of weaving to represent the great mystery of creation and holds special significance for the Vankar community.

Jhini jhini bini chadariya . . .

Kahe ka taana,

Kahe kee bharni . . .

Kaun taar se

bini chadariya . . .

[Who wove this shawl,

So fine, so fine.

What was the warp?

What was the weft?

What was the thread with which

this shawl was woven?

So fine, so fine.]

Bhujodi is one of the biggest handloom clusters in Kutch, home to over 250 weaver families. The Vankar community of weavers has practised their craft for generations, creating beautifully textured shawls, stoles and blankets.

When the weavers work, it's like a symphony—the clatter of the loom, the whirr of the spinning wheel and the splash of the yarns being dunked into dyeing pots. Often, the weavers sing devotional songs or bhajans by Kabir, seamlessly weaving together the familial, cultural, spiritual and historical threads of life in the Vankar community.

THE VANKARS OF KUTCH

The history of the Vankar community of Kutch goes back at least eight hundred years. Originally, the community hailed from Rajasthan and were part of one of the region's oldest nomadic communities, the Meghwals. The Meghwal community had four sub-castes—Maheshwari, Marwada, Gurjara and Chaaran. The Maheshwari and Marwada sub-castes practised weaving fabrics like khadi and working with leather. Placed low in the caste hierarchy, the community faced social exclusion due to their traditional occupation.

The Meghwals originally worshipped nature but, over time, the teachings of the great saints who spoke of an egalitarian world resonated with them deeply. One such revered figure is the twelfth-century saint Veer Meghmaya. It is believed that he sacrificed his life for equal access to clean drinking water as certain communities, including the Meghwals, were denied access to public water sources such as wells and hand pumps.

Another saint revered by the Meghwals is Ramdev Pir, a fourteenth-century Rajput king. He actively opposed discriminatory practices against marginalized communities. The Meghwals were of both Hindu and Muslim ancestry—so, the Hindus called him Ramdev Baba and believed that he was an incarnation of Lord Krishna while the Muslims of the Meghwal community worshipped him as Ramsa or Baba Ramdev Pir.

According to popular legend, Ramdev Pir once went to Narayan Sarovar, a sprawling lake and popular pilgrimage site in Kutch. Some of the saint's followers, who were goldsmiths from the Mandvi region of Kutch, built a few temples in his honour. For the upkeep of these temples, Ramdev Pir invited the weavers of the Meghwal community to Kutch. The Marwada sub-caste of the Meghwal community settled in Bhujodi and the surrounding villages. They transitioned into weaving shawls and blankets and came to be known as the Vankars or weavers while the Maheshwaris settled in Mandvi and started weaving a luscious silk and cotton fabric called *mashru*.

WOVEN STORIES

The Vankars of Kutch weave their story into every shawl, stole or saree they create. The traditional raw materials that they use are sheep and camel yarns and Kala cotton, a variety of short-staple rain-fed cotton indigenous to the region. The colour palette is inspired by nature—lac reds, indigo blues and a range of browns. The classic geometrical motifs that the weavers use are inspired by local architecture, musical instruments and footprints of animal herds.

The Rabaris, an indigenous sheep- and camel-herding community who had migrated to Kutch from Baluchistan thousands of years ago, roamed the desert wetlands. They bartered with other nomadic communities for food and clothing. Skilled in embroidery but lacking weaving expertise, the Rabaris bartered wool, milk and grains with the Vankars in exchange for finely woven shawls.

The Vankar families spent weeks at their looms crafting these patterned shawls that kept the Rabaris warm during chilly nights. The weaves of these unique shawls were so tight that it was said not even a dewdrop could penetrate the garment. When woven loosely, these shawls also provided coolness in the summer.

For over two hundred years, the barter system continued between the Rabaris and the Vankars. The Vankars often followed the nomadic Rabaris, as their livelihood was closely tied to them. The Rabaris' migration patterns, driven by seasons and rainfall, in turn influenced the Vankars' way of life.

Over the last century, however, many Vankars have settled permanently in Bhujodi and the nearby villages, such as Sarli, Adhoi, Kotay and Mota Varnora, to form weaving communities. While the Rabaris are no longer their sole customers, the Vankars' deep-rooted connections with the local communities and their blended cultural ideas continue to shape their traditions. Central to these practices is the music tradition known as Kabir Vaani, which reflects the community's philosophy and connection to the teachings of the revered poet-saint Kabir.

VANKARS AND KABIR VAANI

Here is something interesting about how a culture unfolds. Although succeeding generations often build upon the previous cultures, many times, there is some sort of rebellion against the prevalent culture because of certain fault lines in it. This rebellion is often reflected in the music and art of the new times.

This is exactly what happened during the medieval period in parts of northern India. Because of the caste hierarchies, religion and worship had become highly ritualistic. Lower-caste communities faced discrimination and were barred from entering temples or performing certain religious rituals. The sacred texts, too, were written in a language that could only be read and deciphered by people belonging to the upper castes.

Several poet-saints who lived between the fifteenth and eighteenth centuries believed that religion should not discriminate. People should be able to worship whomever they want; in whatever way they want. This belief led to the Bhakti movement, which laid the foundation for reconfiguring society on a more equitable basis. The poet-saints composed poems and songs devoted to a formless god accessible to all castes. They attacked caste hierarchies, religious divisions, power structures and upper caste strongholds on scriptures while pointing to a greater divinity, a larger truth, within oneself.

While many high-caste individuals dismissed these poet-saints, their songs deeply resonated with marginalized communities. Poets like Kabir and Ravidas, who themselves came from marginalized castes, gave voice to those facing discrimination and exclusion. Their songs provided strength, purpose and dignity, affirming the importance of their work and lives.

For centuries, weaving communities across India have sung Kabir's songs while working. In his verses, Kabir compares weaving to divine creation or likens the human body to a finely woven shawl, using weaving metaphors to simplify complex philosophies. Kabir, from the Julaha or weaver community of Banaras in Uttar Pradesh, is said to have composed these songs while at his loom. Known as Kabir Vaani (the voice of Kabir), these songs spread orally, as Kabir is believed to have been unlettered.

In the folk music tradition of the Vankars of Kutch, Kabir is a living idea. They see him as a powerful guide, a friend and an ally who grapples with many of the issues they face. Over time, his songs have taken on the local colours of the region, growing in a non-textual form purely by being sung and heard as part of the daily routine. These songs reflect the community's philosophy of harmony in contrasts, where two contrasting sets of yarns, *taana-baana* (the warp and the weft), come together to create a beautiful fabric. This philosophy of inclusiveness is deeply integrated into the everyday lives of the Vankars, in ways both seen and unseen. They sing Kabir Vaani to focus their attention on the meticulous details of weaving, to maintain workflow and to underscore the deep association weaving has with many of life's larger truths.

A TWIN TRADITION

In Gujarat, Rajasthan and Madhya Pradesh, as well as in some other parts of India, the tradition of singing Kabir songs thrives in rural settings. There is a parallel tradition of singing songs of the Sufi saints, which share similar themes and metaphors with Kabir Vaani.

The Great Rann of Kutch, for example, is home to the Fakirani Jats, a nomadic pastoral community. For centuries, they have roamed the deserts in search of grazing grounds for their unique kharai camels—that can swim! During the summer and monsoon months, these camels swim to islands in the Gulf of Kutch to feed on marine mangroves.

In the past, the herders journeyed to Sindh (now in Pakistan) across the salt flats of the Great Rann in search of pasture. Though Sindh is now across the border, its cultural impact remains. Sindh and Kutch share deep cultural connections rooted in Sufism, especially in oral folklore, embroidery and visual culture.

A prominent figure in the story of the Fakirani Jats is Bhitai Shah, born Shah Abdul Latif, an eighteenth-century Sufi poet. Despite being a Sayyid, a descendant of Prophet Muhammad, he chose to live humbly as a fakir on a *bhitai* (mound in Sindhi). His profound poems, collected in *Shah Jo Risalo*, are sung by communities across Kutch and Sindh. These poems tell the tales of seven strong female characters, often referred to as the seven queens, and explore themes of eternal love and compassion. Accompanied by the *surando*, a rare five-stringed bowed instrument, the Fakirani Jats have sung the *beth* (songs) of Bhitai Shah for centuries, preserving a common cultural heritage across borders.

Since it possibly took a couple of centuries for Kabir's songs to be written down, the exact details of what he wrote and composed remain uncertain. Consequently, the historicity and authenticity of his poems have often been debated. Kabir's songs have a distinct flavour, a voice that shapes his identity and importance. While the Vankars preserve the essence of the songs, their expansive folk tradition celebrates individual singers and their creative contributions. This ongoing process of creation and recreation enriches the ever-growing canon of Kabir Vaani.

THE ALL-NIGHT SATSANGS

What comes to your mind when you think of the word *satsang*? Perhaps elderly people getting together to sing devotional songs? The Kabir satsangs of the Vankar community, however, are quite different. They are not mere settings for listening to devotional songs but are also spaces for exploration and interrogation.

The Kabir satsangs in the Vankar communities are gatherings where people come together to listen to Kabir Vaani, usually at night after their daily chores and weaving duties are done. These gatherings might take place in village squares, the courtyard of a village temple on special occasions like Ramdev Pir's birth anniversary or *ekadashi* (the eleventh day of a lunar month), or even in people's homes. The songs are typically performed by a group of four to five singers known as bhajan mandalis, who use simple folk instruments such as the dholak, tambura or *ektara*.

These satsangs are more than just singing. They bring alive the philosophies of Kabir. Everyone is welcome to join in and share their thoughts without discrimination. The listeners, therefore, feel a sense of participating in something important, transcending all social limitations. These satsangs keep the spirit of music and the joy of singing alive while forging deeper connections within the community.

ART AIDING ART

Have you ever wondered about how the fabric for your clothes was made or how a basket or rug was created? Weaving is one of the oldest crafts, dating back at least 12,000 years. Early humans used branches and twigs to make homes, baskets and other useful objects. Throughout history, humans have acknowledged the musicality of weaving and weaving communities across the globe sing while they weave. In fact, weaving songs are mentioned in ancient texts such as the Rigveda, the world's oldest Sanskrit writings, as well as Homer's Greek epic, The Odyssey.

THE SUFIYANA KALAM OF KASHMIR

In Kashmir, the carpet-making communities practice Sufiyana kalam, a musical form linked to Sufi saints. This tradition has been passed down orally through generations. During weaving, the lead weaver sings out patterns for others to follow, using rhythm to communicate with fellow weavers. *Mehfils* (night-long musical gatherings) featuring Sufi songs were once a common part of the *karkhanas* (weaving centres) in the Valley.

THE WEAVING SONGS OF THE CHANGPAS OF LADAKH

Some folk traditions invoke the myths of divine beings teaching humans to spin thread, or gods bestowing humans with the gift of looms. Among these is the nomadic Changpa community from Ladakh's Changthang plateau, known for their pashmina shawls. Both men and women weave on portable looms, but only women use backstrap looms. A local myth connects their weaving practice to the magical loom of Duguma, wife of the mythical Buddhist king Gesar of Ling, who weaves a row each year, with the world ending when her fabric is complete. In their songs, aspects of weaving symbolize Buddhist philosophy and practice.

THE TRINJAN SONGS OF PUNJAB

In the villages of Punjab, women gather in open courtyards during the day to spin cotton, chat and sing. This practice, known as *trinjan*, provides rhythm to their spinning and reflects their lives and culture. Many trinjan express the hopes, desires and sorrows of women. The night trinjan is called *rat katni* and the day trinjan is known as *chiri charoonga*.

A LIVING TRADITION

The many oral traditions of Kabir Vaani have flourished through the voices of ordinary people who sing them and find deep meaning in their lyrics. The Vankar community of Kutch uniquely intertwines the act of weaving with Kabir's philosophies, creating a folk music tradition rich in metaphor and melody.

In today's divisive times, the Vankars' folk music continues to sing of Kabir's 'Jhini Bini Chadariya', the interlacement of the warp and the weft for the creation of a finely woven cloth—bringing two seemingly opposite ideas into harmony. This offers a profound insight into the worldview of the Vankar community, which recognizes differences without perceiving them as threatening. Instead, they view these differences as central to the creation of a beautiful tapestry of ideas.

As our world increasingly emphasizes borders and rigid identities, the Vankar community's songs remain a powerful celebration of diversity—the reason why we need these songs today more than ever.

LISTENING LISTS:

Search words: Kabir Bhajan, Kabir Vaani, The Kabir Project, Bhujodi Bhajan Mandali, Ajab Shahar, Prahlad Singh Tipaniya, Shabnam Virmani

1. A rendition of a Kabir bhajan by the singer Bijal Meghwal. https://www.youtube.com/watch?v=HY2mPaebqbs

2. A Kabir bhajan by Bhujodi Bhajan Mandali. https://www.youtube.com/watch?v=xO_p5l4G3ew

3. A rendition of Kabir's 'Chadariya Jheeni Re Jheeni' by Mukhtiyar Ali, an extraordinary performer of Sufiana kalam and bhakti songs. https://www.youtube.com/watch?v=7z9dM2E1Zl8

4. A soulful rendition of 'Thaara Rang Mahal Mein' by Prahlad Singh Tipanya, one of India's foremost folk singers of Kabir's poetry. https://www.youtube.com/watch?v=cApx92qpFks

5. Filmmaker and singer Shabnam Virmani performs Kabir's compositions at Jashn-e-Rekhta. https://www.youtube.com/watch?v=wpGOMJPZges

SONGS FROM THE MARGINS

The Janapadas of the Jogappas of Karnataka

About five kilometres from the sleepy town of Saundatti, on the Karnataka-Maharashtra border, atop the sacred hill of Yellamma Guddu overlooking the Malaprabha river, stands an ancient temple believed to have been built in the sixteenth century by Bomappa Nayak, the king of Raybag.

The presiding deity is Yellamma, also known as Renuka, whose idol is enshrined in the dark inner sanctum of the temple. Depicted seated and draped in a red saree, Yellamma is adorned with bangles on her right hand and holds a bunch of neem leaves in her left.

Every year, on the full-moon night of Margasira, the ninth month of the Hindu-Kannada calendar, lakhs of devotees flock to the temple for the Yellamma jatra. During this festival, the quaint town of Saundatti transforms into a bustling fairground. Streets leading to the temple are lined with makeshift stalls selling fruits and flowers, sarees and soaps, glass bangles and garlands. Thick crowds of devotees wait to offer their naivaidyams *(ritual offerings to the goddess).*

In this vibrant scene, the Jogappas—a community of devotees integral to the jatra—play a central role. Among India's oldest and least-known transgender communities, they are believed to serve as intermediaries between the goddess and the people. Dressed in colourful sarees, adorned with cowrie necklaces and with haldi-kumkum smeared on their foreheads, the Jogappas sing janapadas—*songs in praise of goddess Yellamma rooted in the larger folkloric tradition of the region.*

India's transgender communities have a varied history. From revered figures in Hindu mythology to influential political advisors in the Mughal courts and marginalized groups during British rule, these communities have played diverse roles throughout history.

The term 'transgender' broadly encompasses individuals who are either born intersex, with physical attributes differing from conventional male and female categories, or those whose gender identity, expression and behaviour do not conform to those typically associated with the sex assigned at birth. Within this spectrum, various sub-cultures such—as *hijras, kothis, aravanis* and *shiv-shaktis*—have their own specific rituals, traditions and even languages. This array of practices and beliefs highlights the richness of their contributions to the cultural landscape of India.

THE JOGAPPAS: OFFERED TO THE GODDESS

The Jogappas live in the rural areas along the borders of Karnataka, Maharashtra and Telangana, dedicating their lives to the service of goddess Yellamma. According to age-old practices, when an individual—often from a lower caste—identifies as transgender and experiences

THE MYTH OF AN ACCIDENTAL GODDESS

Many mythical tales about goddess Yellamma's origin exist in oral traditions. One popular story goes like this:

In the Sahyadri Hills by the Bhagirathi river, there once lived a king named Renukaraja and his wife Bhogawatidev. They longed for a child. After years of observing fasts, performing rituals and praying incessantly, they were blessed with a baby girl whom they named Renuka, derived from the word *renuvu* (the finest grain of sand).

As Renuka grew into a beautiful woman, kings from far and wide sought her hand in marriage. However, she fell in love with the sage Jamdagni, one of the *saptarishis* (seven great sages) and chose to live with him in his humble home. They had five sons, including Parasurama, the sixth reincarnation of Vishnu.

Renuka, known for her wifely virtues, possessed magical powers to carry water in unbaked pots. One day, while fetching water from the river, she saw Chitrangada, the celestial king, and admired him from afar. Her magical pot dissolved, drenching her in the water.

While appreciating someone's beauty may seem a natural and inoffensive matter to our modern sensibility, clearly the ancients, at least in this story, saw things differently. When Renuka returned home, Jamdagni realized she had lost her powers and deduced that she had 'faltered'. The enraged Jamdagni commanded his sons to behead Renuka. While four of his sons refused, (clearly, they were the sensible ones), Parasurama eventually obeyed and beheaded Renuka with an axe given by Lord Shiva.

Parasurama received a boon for his obedience while his brothers lost their masculinity. He asked for his mother's resurrection, but her head was missing. Only after replacing it with another woman's head did Renuka return to life as Yellamma, a goddess revered by those shunned by society.

The story varies a great deal from this point. One popular version says Renuka's original head multiplied and fell at various places, becoming shrines, with her four sons becoming priests. Major temples dedicated to Yellamma are in Mahur in Maharashtra, and Saundatti, Chandraguthi and Hulgi in Karnataka.

Carrying the severed head of the goddess, it is believed, raises one above the earthly plane. So, the Jogappas carry small, portable shrines of Yellamma, represented by a metal head attached to the rim of a basket or a pot, on their heads as they go from house to house in the designated villages seeking alms and singing songs to spread the glory of the goddess.

inexplicable ailments such as fits or skin rashes, or possesses a distinctive dreadlock known as a *jatey*, it is interpreted as a divine call to join the Jogappa tradition. Ignoring these signs is seen as defying divine will. So, these individuals, often pressurized by their families but sometimes acting of their own accord, give up everything to serve the goddess.

The families offer the child to goddess Yellamma through a ritual called *muttu kattodu*. After undergoing a ceremonial marriage to the deity, male-born transgenders become a part of the close group of attendants of the goddess and are known as the *jogappas* or *jogtas* (the female-born devotees are called *jogatis*). The jogappas adopt characteristics that are traditionally associated with women, such as shaving off their moustaches and beards, growing their hair long and wearing colourful sarees and ornate jewellery. They also wear a distinctive nuptial thread crafted with red-and-white beads known as the *muthu*. A senior jogappa usually ties the muthu around the newly initiated jogappa's neck and becomes their guru. The guru and the jogappa share a mother–daughter relationship. Once initiated, jogappas are prohibited from marrying, having a biological family or holding positions of office outside the dedicated roles in Yellamma worship.

THE REBEL WITH A CAUSE

The jogappa practice, steeped in superstitious beliefs and normalized for centuries, was first questioned by Tukaram Bhaurao Sathe, popularly known as Annabhau Sathe, in the early twentieth century. A great social reformer, folk poet and writer from Maharashtra, he produced an extensive commentary on caste- and gender-based injustices in his works. Known as the father of Dalit literature, he began writing at a time when novels, short stories and plays were predominantly created by the upper castes. Many of his works describe the alienation faced by socially excluded communities such as the Jogappas and serve as unique tools for understanding their everyday realities.

VERSATILE MUSICIANS

The jogappas typically make a living through *joga,* which includes begging, singing and dancing. After their initiation, they receive training in traditional music from their guru. They perform at temples dedicated to goddess Yellamma, for gatherings of devotees from nearby villages, or are invited to sing at auspicious occasions such as births and weddings.

Some jogappas carry a handcrafted straw basket or brass and copper pots containing the idol of the goddess, called the *pardi* and travel from village to village. They sing hymns and seek alms. Failure to offer them alms is considered an invitation of the goddess's wrath, manifesting as deaths, failed crops or debts. This belief places jogappas in a sacred role within the community, where people seek their blessings to appease the goddess.

Jogappas mainly sing bhajans in local dialects such as Kannada, Marathi and Telugu. These songs often begin with a melodic line sung by a lead singer, followed by a chorus to help the audience follow along. Many of the songs recount the myths of Yellamma in her various forms and celebrate her victory over patriarchal norms. For example:

> *Messe mattu kasse iddavara,*
> *Solisi seere udisidavalu Yellamma.*
> *Bhaviyu bhaviyaagi bandavara,*
> *Baayalli baagina neeridavalu Yellamma.*
> [Those who sport moustaches and wear lungis,
> Yellamma makes them wear a saree.
> Those who come with devotion and love,
> Yellamma fills their mouths with sweet blessings.]

In addition to devotional songs, the Jogappas have a diverse repertoire covering themes such as love, lifecycle events and social issues. They sing in a high-pitched, devotion-charged voice for long hours, accompanied by three instruments—the *chowdki*, a rhythmic stringed instrument with an open wooden drum; the *sutti*, similar to an ektara for maintaining pitch; and the *taal*, a pair of tiny cymbals.

Considered to be a symbol of goddess Yellamma, chowdki is a rare percussion instrument that is estimated to be around 2,500 years old. A single-stringed instrument, it has a cylindrical drum made of bark and covered with animal hide on one side. It has a wooden arm close to its mouth. A metal piece is inserted through a hole in the centre of the sheathed part and a string is tied between the bamboo and the hide. It is attached to the peg on top of the instrument. The sound is produced by plucking the string with fingers or with a small rod that has tiny bells attached on either side.

The chowdki gets its name from the sound it makes and is usually played with the sutti, a hollow drum with a long handle. In the Jogappa tradition, the sutti is seen as a male instrument and the chowdki as its female counterpart, reflecting the concept of combined male-female energies. Both instruments are believed to produce pitch-perfect music only when played together. However, due to social stigmatization, these instruments are now on the verge of extinction, with few remaining players.

JOGATHI NRITYA

The transgender people of the Jogappa tradition perform a high-energy folk dance called the *jogathi nritya*. This ritual dance, featuring songs dedicated to the goddess Yellamma, has become an integral part of Karnataka's folk art. To the sounds of the chowdki and sutti, the performers move gracefully while wearing an imposing headgear—a metal-crafted idol of Yellamma inside a pot. They swing their waists and sway their hands with abandon, yet in perfect rhythm with the devotional songs. Buoyed by years of practice, the performers execute eye-catching stunts such as bending backward, rotating and pirouetting, picking up coins from the floor using just the mouth—all while balancing a pot on their heads!

MUSIC OF THE TRANSGENDER COMMUNITIES

Many transgender communities across India perform music and dance in various styles and use them to construct or negotiate their identities.

MENZIMYEORS OF KASHMIR: Traditionally a matchmaker community, the Menzimyeor transpeople are known for their beautiful *bach-e-nagmeh* (ceremonial folk song and dance) performed at weddings.

PAVAIYAS OF GUJARAT: Worshippers of Bahuchara Mata, an incarnation of Shakti or the divine feminine, the Pavaiyas sing and dance at auspicious events such as weddings and births, or trade events such as store openings. Their songs invoke the goddess and also highlight their role as spiritual intermediaries between the goddess and her devotees.

HIJRAS OF NORTH INDIA: The hijras, a queer minority, typically sing *badhais* or songs of felicitation at ceremonial occasions, such as births or weddings. Their performances are often accompanied by their distinctive hijra clap, where palms strike perpendicularly with fingers splayed. A hijra *toli* or group usually consists of two to six individuals, including a lead singer, supporting singers and a dholak player.

NUPI MANBI OF MANIPUR: Many transgender women perform to the loud rhythmic beats of Manipur's traditional *thabal chongba*, a folk dance associated with Yaosang or the spring festival.

During the Dussehra season, the Jogappas perform a ritualistic overnight play called the *Yellammanaata* (the play of goddess Yellamma), which retells the myth of Renuka and her transformation into the powerful goddess. Originally, the Jogappa priests of the Yellamma temple narrated this story as a *nata* (street play) which later evolved into a staged performance. These days, with support from the government and NGOs, these performances also serve as a medium for conveying social messages, particularly to rural women.

THE DANCING QUEEN

Jogathi nritya, as it is known today, owes much of its identity and popularity to one of the foremost exponents of this dance form, Manjamma Jogathi.

In 1957, in the Kallukamba village near Bellary, Karnataka, a baby was born to Hanumantaiah and Jayalakshmi, a middle-class couple who had lost seventeen of their twenty-one children. The baby was named Manjunatha Shetty.

As Manjunatha grew into a young boy, he liked doing ordinary things that boys his age did, like going to school and playing, but he also realized that he was quite unlike them. At fifteen, he felt his body was at odds with his gender identity—he identified as a girl and enjoyed doing things that he had seen girls in his community do. This difference led to frequent bullying. The boys in his neighbourhood would pinch him, pull his hair and box his ears at the slightest provocation.

Manjunatha's only moments of joy came when he borrowed his female friends' long skirts and blouses to dance to Kannada film songs. When his parents discovered this, they sent him to live with his brother in the village, but the situation did not improve.

In Manjunatha's community, transgender children were traditionally offered to goddess Yellamma through a ritual and his fate was no different. He became Manjamma Jogathi, bound to serve the goddess with no chance of returning home. Abandoned and humiliated, Manjamma had no choice but to beg on the streets to survive.

When Manjamma was about twenty, one day, while seeking alms at a bus stand in Davanagere, she heard the hypnotic sound of a chowdki and saw a large crowd gathered at some distance. She headed there in the hope of receiving alms. As she got closer, she saw a man playing the chowdki and a young boy with long, plaited hair dancing with a pot on his head. Mesmerized by the boy's performance, Manjamma approached the man, shared her story and asked, 'Appaji, I want to dance like this boy. Can you teach me?' The man replied, 'You can watch your *tamma* (younger brother) and learn.'

That night, filled with excitement, Manjamma couldn't sleep. With a small pot on her head, she kept moving around her hut. From the next day, she followed the duo, Appaji and his son Parasurama, wherever they went. She observed the boy's dance and tried to memorize all the moves. Once home, Manjamma practised the moves with a pot on her head. Soon, Manjamma was travelling from village to village with Appaji and Parasurama and performing.

After about a year, Manjamma joined a group of dancers who were much respected in the region. During this time, a member of the group introduced her to Guru Kalavva Jogathi of Hagaribommanahalli, a folk artist whose troupe was performing in Manjamma's village. Kalavva invited her to join his troupe. Under Kalavva's mentorship, Manjamma mastered the performance of *Yellammanaata*. She also brought jogathi nritya to the stage. She performed extensively across the state and, after Kalavva's death, took over the troupe, and continued to perform to further popularize the dance form.

In 2019, Manjamma became the first transgender woman appointed as the chairperson of the Karnataka Janapada Academy, a cultural academy dedicated to the study of folklore. In 2021, she was honoured with the Padma Shri for her contribution to folk art. As sexual minorities across India continue to fight for their rights and acceptance, Manjamma Jogathi's life stands as a shining example of resilience and achievement.

THE UNSUNG MUSICIANS

The word 'transgender' might have been coined in the early twentieth century, but in India, transgenders have been known for hundreds of years by different names. They have had an all-pervasive existence across all classes, races and castes and have conventionally been associated with music and dance. Yet, they have never been considered important artists whose contributions to Indian arts have been acknowledged or recognized.

When we take a closer look at history and how rituals were constructed, songs composed and dances performed, we observe how structures of social hierarchy present themselves—and these hierarchies, for the longest time, have governed who gets to be seen as an artist and what is considered art. The Jogappas is one such community of musicians, dancers and performers who have been marginalized, a community that has been overlooked in 'mainstream' musical narratives of India.

FROM THE MARGINS TO THE MAINSTREAM

One of the first efforts to re-contextualize Jogappa music from the streets and on to the public stage was made by Carnatic vocalist, composer and author T.M. Krishna in 2017. In a series of performances, Krishna collaborated with five Jogappa singers and, through music, tried to look beyond the boundaries of caste and gender, folk and classical, and rural and urban.

Though the Jogappa tradition was born out of a patriarchal context steeped in complex myths, religious beliefs and local superstitions, their music remains one of India's finest folk traditions. While their current reality might not indicate this, as many Jogappa musicians continue to perform on the streets, they are skilled artists, with years of hard work and training behind them. Their music, still relatively unacknowledged, tends to tell many stories that have been ignored or erased for centuries. These are the stories we must seek out now more than ever, because the inclusivity of our world depends on whose stories are heard and whose are ignored.

LISTENING LIST:

Search words: Jogappas, Jogathi Nritya, Chowdki, Shruti, Manjamma Jogathi, Urban Folk Project, Shilpa Mudbi

1. A one-of-a-kind concert where Carnatic music maestro T.M. Krishna shared the stage with Jogappa singers.
   https://www.youtube.com/watch?v=QsHbt6rtXiA

2. Part 2 of the unique concert featuring Carnatic music maestro T.M. Krishna and Jogappa singers.
   https://www.youtube.com/watch?v=vnOCXc3hrR4

3. A Sahapedia video exploring the role of chowdki and sutti in the Jogathi community's music and rituals.
   https://www.youtube.com/watch?v=eZsyl8FSdRI

4. A Jogathi Nritya performance by Manjamma Jogathi and others.
   https://www.youtube.com/watch?v=w2dukKnpiHo

5. 'Yellamma and Other Stories', a performance by Urban Folk Project at Bangalore Literature Festival 2018.
   https://www.youtube.com/watch?v=S8M_BdZDkzw

SONGS OF LIBERATION

The Lavani Folk Music of Maharashtra

The stage is set. The excitement in the audience is palpable. The foot-tapping beat of the dholki *(a small high-pitched folk drum) reverberates around the hall complemented by the rich tones of the harmonium.*

A heavily bejewelled, nauvari-saree-clad *dancer makes her entrance, with the loose end of her saree draped over her head, partly covering her face. She glides across the stage as the innumerable plum-sized ghunghroos tied to her ankles make a chham-chham sound with each step. She sways and stops at the centre of the stage. Then, with a practised flourish, she lifts her veil to the sound of the song:*

> *Apsara aali, Indrapuritun khali.*
>
> *Pasarali laali, ratnaprabhatun lyali.*
>
> *Ti hasali gaali, chandani rangmahali.*
>
> [A celestial nymph has descended from Indra's abode.
>
> Spreading her radiance, she's like a bejewelled dawn.
>
> Her moonlit smile has illuminated the stage of the earth.]

After bowing to the audience with three rapid scoops of her hand, the dancer tosses her head sideways, arches her eyebrows and flutters her eyelids—causing the audience to erupt in loud roars.

This is a snippet of a performance from a centuries-old folk music and dance form from Maharashtra called *lavani*. Performed by dancers dressed in bright nine-yard sarees and elaborate jewellery, lavani is a combination of narrative songs sung in quick tempo to the beats of dholki and dynamic dance sequences.

Derived from the Sanskrit word *lavanya*, meaning beauty, the origins of lavani are uncertain. Some thirteenth-century texts suggest that the folk form originated in the nomadic Kolhati or rope-walking community of Maharashtra, whose traditional profession was dancing and entertainment. However, it was only in the seventeenth and eighteenth centuries that lavani blossomed into a performative art form under the patronage of Maratha rulers and gained popularity in Maharashtra, Madhya Pradesh, Gujarat and along the Konkan coast.

Lavani was traditionally performed by fiesty, expressive women dancers in *baithak*s (sit-down performances) for patrons, with songs marked by robust ribaldry and themes centred around women. Unlike traditional dance forms, none of the moves in lavani are fixed— they are improvised to elicit the desired response from the audience. The dancers own the stage and, with a twitch of a lip, a twirl of the hands or a wink of the eye, establish an immediate connection with the audience. It is this relationship that the performers establish with the audience that defines the electrifying energy of the lavani performances.

This agile folk song-and-dance form not only explores and celebrates various forms of love, beauty and pleasure but also presents commentary on the social and cultural complexities. Despite its long history, lavani remains grossly marginalized and often misrepresented. To fully appreciate this art form's place in history, it is important to examine its roots and evolution.

THE ORIGINS OF LAVANI

The songs of lavani are believed to have their roots in the *Gatha Saptashati*, a collection of seven hundred verses written in Prakrit and composed by the seventeenth king of the Satavahana dynasty, Hala, in the second century CE about the everyday experiences of the people. Although the *Gatha Saptashati* is essentially a compilation of love poetry that reflects the rural life and culture of Maharashtra, some of its gathas—written as couplets and delightfully naughty in tone—bear a close structural and thematic resemblance to lavani songs. Hence, some scholars suggest that these gathas could be precursors to lavani.

It was during the Maratha rule in the seventeenth century that lavani took on its distinct form. This period saw the emergence of a tradition of prose writing in the form of historic narratives known as *bakhars*. These narratives, mainly biographies of great rulers or accounts of significant battles, were complemented by a poetic tradition of popular history called *shahiri kavan*. The composer-singers of this form of poetry were called *shahirs* (poets). The related genres of *powadas* (historical ballads) and lavanis (love songs) were a significant part of their work.

Initially, lavani had two branches—the *nirguni* lavani with philosophical, spiritual undertones and the *shringari* lavani, which focused on sensual themes. While the nirguni lavani was popular in the Malwa region of west-central India, it gradually fell into obscurity. But the shringari lavani, thrived in the following centuries as the shahirs started receiving patronage from the Maratha rulers such as the Holkars of Indore and the Bhonsles of Tanjore, both great aficionados of music and literature.

By the turn of the eighteenth century, lavani reached the pinnacle of its popularity during the Peshwa rule, centred in Pune. The expansion of the Maratha empire under the Peshwas led to increased demand for entertainment, particularly for war-weary soldiers. Lavani performances, staged by female dancers—often slaves from lower caste communities such as Kolhati, Bhatu, Kalwat, Mahar, Matangi and Dombari—were held exclusively for male audiences at the royal courts. These dancers, trained in singing and dancing at state-sponsored *natakshalas* (performance schools), became a crucial part of the entertainment.

Lavani performances comprised two components—the poetry and the performance. While female dancers led the performance, the poetry was predominantly written by men. The narratives in these songs focused on women's experiences, characterized by themes of love, desire and longing borne out of separation from the beloved due to military campaigns. These emotionally charged songs were marked by their rhythmic quality and lucid language. The poets defied the conventions of classical Marathi poetry, grounding their expression in the everyday lives of people. These performances provided for soldiers a magical respite from the miseries of war.

As the years went by, the performances became increasingly elaborate with bright costumes and ornate jewellery. Historians record that in the eighteenth century, during the reign of the Peshwa king Balaji Baji Rao, a fifty-two-room, double-storey tenement called Bavankhani was built in Pune, with rooms rented out to women performers. Gradually, lavani came to be appreciated not only by royalty but also by other powerful and affluent men. Intimate gatherings were held by rich patrons, including traders, landlords and local nobles and the performers sang and danced predominantly in a sitting position. This style came to be known as the *baithakaichi* lavani (lavani performed while sitting down).

TAMASHA, THE TRAVELLING THEATRE

With the fall of the Peshwas and the rise of the British empire in the early nineteenth century, the royal patronage for lavani came to an end. By that time, however, this unique song-and-dance form had firmly established itself in public consciousness.

This period also saw the rise in popularity of *tamasha* (rural theatre). Tamasha performances were typically held at village fairs, weekly markets and *bail bazaars* (buffalo markets) by *natak mandalis* (travelling troupes). Each troupe comprised of a bunch of versatile actors, singers, dancers and music accompanists. A typical tamasha performance included five segments: *gan*, an opening prayer to Lord Ganesha; *gvalan*, a dance based on the interaction between Krishna and the *gopis; baatvani*, a funny or sarcastic interaction between the comperes; *rangbazi,* a dance medley and *vag nritya,* a folk drama. But in all these components, cross-dressed men performed the female parts, as it was socially unacceptable for women to perform in public at that time.

THE WHOLE NINE YARDS

Lavani dancers usually wear a *nauvari* saree, which is nine yards long. It is draped in the distinctive *kashta* style, which means the saree is tucked at the back, like a dhoti. The dancer's hair is tied in a bun called *ambada* with flowers woven around it. The accessories worn by the dancers include *kamar patta* (waistband), earrings, necklace, bangles and a *nath* (nose ring). The dancers also tie ghungroos or anklet bells. Each of these *ghungroos* weigh around four kilograms. Because of their weight, the ghungroos create a loud sound and were especially useful for tamasha performances, which were performed in the open areas without sophisticated sound systems.

However, things began to change when one of the greatest *lok shahirs,* Patthe Bapurao, encouraged his wife to perform in tamashas. Bapurao, who had written numerous lavanis presented by the performers of his time, was married to a lavani dancer, Pauda Bai. He brought her to the tamasha stage to perform one of the lavanis he had written for the rangbazi segment. This marked a new chapter in lavani's history in the 1870s, as many lavani performers began performing in public.

Soon, lavani came to be integrated with tamasha and was now performed for a wider Marathi-speaking audience. This form of lavani came to be known as the *dholki phadacha* tamasha, which included song, dance and theatre. Unlike the lavani performed in a baithak format, the performers in dholki phadacha tamasha used the entire stage. They travelled to villages, lived in tents and performed for eight months every year. During the monsoon months, travel was halted. So, to provide work for these performers all through the year, many theatres opened in Maharashtra where tamashas began to be staged.

Apart from popular entertainment, tamashas also started exploring social issues and raising awareness. Topics such as unemployment, dowry and addiction were addressed. Tamashas on themes of colonial rule and patriotism were also in demand, especially during the independence movement.

THE ROOTED FORM

Alongside the dholki phadaichi tamasha, which served as an inexpensive medium of popular entertainment, another genre of lavani called the *sangeet barichi* tamasha evolved as a part of the baithakaichi lavani tradition. This form was more focused on song and dance than theatre and was performed in intimate settings for small groups. These performances were unabashedly sensual in appeal and often violated conventional notions of propriety.

While the dholki phadaichi troupes consisted numerous artists who travelled in trucks and buses to different places, the sangeet barichi troupes were much smaller, with performers who lived and performed in theatres. Traditionally, these groups only had female performers, mainly from the Kolhati or Kalwaat communities and were barred by their caste from marrying. The troupe or 'sangeet party' was usually owned by a woman and the performers lived in an almost matriarchal set-up. The performers and the owner worked in a partnership, each entitled to a fixed share of the profits.

Sangeet barichi performances operated on a patronage basis for an exclusive audience. The zestful performances were characterized by direct, playful interaction with the audience. Through their singing and dancing, the performers pushed the audiences out of their comfort zone. They danced to audience requests and their impromptu repartee laced with wit and humour was the highlight of the performances.

Since each theatre could accommodate seven to eight sangeet parties at a time, the groups performed in rotation every evening, creating a highly competitive environment. If one troupe received an enthusiastic response for their performance, the next day's troupe faced the challenge of surpassing their success. To meet these high expectations, performers dedicated themselves to rigorous training. They would first study the lavani in detail, memorize its lyrics and develop a range of gestures to convey each word. They then focused on perfecting their singing and choreography. As a result, lavani flourished and soon many *kala kendras* (art centres) or *sangeet bari* theatres opened across Maharashtra. Even today, various groups of sangeet bari performers continue to live and perform together for select audiences.

THE CHANGING GRAMMAR

Although the folk form of lavani has been a cultural mainstay in Maharashtra for ages, it has had a tumultuous history. Due to its bold content and sensual appeal, it has long been frowned upon. In 1948, the then chief minister, Balasaheb Kher, imposed a ban on tamasha performances, deeming them 'immoral' and 'inappropriate' for public consumption. With their means of livelihood under threat, the performers came together and wrote a petition to the government, detailing how the survival of tamasha and lavani is important for the survival of many artists. After negotiations, the ban was lifted, but tamasha performances were subjected to new regulations. A tamasha board was established to approve all performances, including lavani, before they could be presented to the public. The censorship of the art form led to the reimagining of the lavani to 'make it suitable' for public entertainment, causing a paradigm shift in its writing and performance and resulting in sanitization of many standard tropes.

Over time, cinema became a popular source of entertainment. This, coupled with the shutting down of many theatres due to the real-estate boom, led to lavani making its way into the movies and reality shows. However, this modern form of lavani—the one that most people associate the folk form with—is a watered-down version of the traditional one.

In the early 1990s, driven by a renewed interest in regional cultures and the growing influence of Marathi films which began to feature lavani performances, this folk form became popular again. As societal attitudes shifted, lavani gained recognition, leading many urban troupes to perform it on stage like any other performing art form. Professionally trained dancers started delivering three-hour shows at ticketed venues, accompanied by live music. One of the most important changes that these shows brought was the entry of performers from the many different communities not traditionally associated with lavani. These shows brought down the caste barriers and experimented with stories and styles. Each troupe developed its own grammar of lavani and distinct way of performing it. This led to many diverse ideas about what lavani meant in the modern era. These urban troupes collectively came to be known as 'banner shows'.

RECLAIMING A FOLK FORM

With time, each art form creates its own mutations and the same is true for lavani. Today, it exists across Maharashtra and is constantly reinventing itself. It is no longer just tales of war-wrought separation; it now addresses a wide range of themes, including gender equality, illiteracy, farmer suicides, dowry deaths, demonetization and elections. Ironically, while lavani has been an important part of the cultural fabric of western India for many centuries and its content has now been somewhat censored, its performers still face stigmatization and marginalization.

Historically, lavani was composed by and performed for men by women performers from oppressed communities. The intersection of class and caste vulnerabilities, coupled with the bold expression of femininity in their song and dance, led to lavani performers being labelled 'immoral' over time. This has denied lavani a rightful place in the country's performing arts landscape and excluded its feisty, highly skilled performers from the cultural mainstream.

DANCING THROUGH THE STEREOTYPES

When women took the song-and-dance form to the public stage, the men who crossed-dressed and performed slowly fell out of favour. The last decade, however, has seen the return of cross-dressing performers. In 2000, Mumbai's first all-male lavani dance troupe called Bin Baykancha Tamasha (a tamasha without women) was formed. This troupe allowed men to take up the traditionally women-centric dance form, making it more inclusive. Without the exaggeration or mockery that often characterizes cross-dressed characters in cinema, these performances became a celebration of femininity in all its beauty and complexity.

While the system in which lavani germinated was deeply exploitative, this unique performance art form is, in itself, an empowering expression of feminine energy. Once on stage, the performers assert their individuality and claim agency by taking charge of their interaction with the audience. They look back at them and, in doing so, subvert the public gaze. They break through layers of social and cultural stigma by pushing the audience to question their notions of right and wrong, proper and improper, good and bad. And, in this way, they take forward the tradition of lavani as a living, liberating art form.

LISTENING LIST:

Search words: Lavani Songs, Baithakaichi Lavani, Dholki Phadaichi Tamasha, Sangeet Barichi, Gauri Jadhav, Akshay Malvankar

1. The song 'Apsara Aali' from the Marathi movie *Natarang*. Veteran music composer duo Ajay-Atul composed the original score for the film.
   https://www.youtube.com/watch?v=mW67u_hWiSo

2. A recording of the thematic concert baithakaichi lavani, conceptualized and music directed by Dr Ashok Da Ranade, the pioneer of cultural musicology, at Pulotsav, Pune, in November 1999.
   https://www.youtube.com/watch?v=yk1Kk9a35qQ

3. A captivating lavani performance by renowned artist Gauri Jadhav.
   https://www.youtube.com/watch?v=6llMbv5kJuw

4. An energetic performance by the lavani artist Akshay Malvankar.
   https://www.youtube.com/watch?v=mMwmAOEb-8k

5. An exploration of desire and consent through lavani by Agents of Ishq, an online multi-media project that seeks to create a space for public discourse on sex and sexuality in India.
   https://youtu.be/TLsqNCzSkZQ?si=w415Z8RJ-zS-HqpQ

SONGS OF THE BLUE HILLS

The Li of the Chakhesang Nagas

Clusters of gable-roofed houses. Emerald-green paddy fields. Babbling brooks and rushing streams. The picture postcard village of Khezhakano, or Kozabomi, is nestled in the blue hills of Phek district in the northeastern state of Nagaland. One of the village's most intriguing wonders, however, is a magnificent spirit stone called Tsotawo, which is central to the legend of the land and traces the magical beginnings of many Naga tribes.

According to the oral history of the Nagas, the first Naga chief was an old man named Koza who came from the eastern parts of the world to the Naga Hills. He and his wife Kola-O, along with their three sons and pet mithun, travelled relentlessly for days and nights until they reached Mekroma in Manipur. There, they rested and prayed to Chukichi-O, the supreme creator, to guide their way. Suddenly, a kite alighted on the horn of the mithun and then flew off in the direction of a place called Khezhakano.

Koza placed his walking stick on the ground and it pointed in the same direction the bird had flown. When Koza tried to pick up his stick, he could not—it had turned into a pear tree! Koza took it as guidance from the spirits and set off in that direction.

When they reached Khezhakano, they saw the same kite that Koza had seen earlier, now perched on a slab of stone. Then, a frog appeared on the stone with a stalk of paddy in its mouth. When Koza removed the stalk from the frog's mouth and placed it on the stone, it doubled itself to Koza's utter amazement. It was a spirit stone, Koza realized. All the signs indicated that Koza and his family should settle down there. He made Khezhakano his home and started cultivating paddy.

Legend has it that when Koza dried his paddy on the spirit stone, it doubled by the afternoon. Every day, Koza's three sons took turns drying their share of the paddy on the magic stone. But, over time, jealousy crept in between the brothers and the two elder brothers prevented their younger brother from drying his paddy on the stone. Seeing the brothers' frequent quarrels, Kola-O became deeply worried that if this continued, they would kill each other over the magic stone. So, she decided to destroy the stone.

One fateful day, she asked one of her sons to get some dry sesame. She placed it beneath the stone and set it on fire. With the heat, the stone cracked and a dove ascended from it towards heaven. The stone lost its magic.

After this, the three sons decided to go their separate ways. The eldest son, followed by some people from the village, moved to Kohima and formed the Angami tribe. The second son, along with others, moved to the Zunheboto district and formed the Sumi tribe. The youngest one decided to stay back in the village with the remaining population and formed the Chakhesang tribe (the name derived from the first syllables of three sub-tribes, namely Chokri, Kheza and Sangtam). And thus, the village of Khezhakano came to be inhabited by the Chakhesang tribe.

Like all the seventeen tribes in Nagaland, the Chakhesangs have a rich folk heritage, with a story for every stone, a song for every river and a legend for each corner of the land. In a community where orality is still significant, these stories and songs are passed on through word of mouth from one generation to the next.

The Chakhesang tribe has a unique tradition of folk songs sung in a dialect called Chokri, which has an estimated 20,000 speakers. These community songs cover all reasons and seasons—the mystical allure of Nagaland, the agrarian lifestyle, the praise of ancient warriors and folk heroes, love songs, lullabies and songs of mourning and loss. This rich tradition of folk songs is known as *li*, literally meaning the songs of the people and their land.

THE CHAKHESANGS

We often assume that Nagaland simply means the land of the Nagas. However, the Nagas are not a single tribe but comprise over sixty-four different tribes (with many sub-tribes). Each tribe speaks its own language, follows distinct customs and traditions and wears tribe-specific attire. Seventeen of these tribes reside within the borders of Nagaland, while the rest are spread across Manipur, Arunachal Pradesh, Assam and even Myanmar.

The origins of the diverse tribes of Nagaland have been a subject of great debate among scholars and historians. To this day, it has not been conclusively established where the different Naga tribes came from and how are they related to one another. The general consensus is that the Nagas are Indo-Mongoloid by race, who came to the Naga Hills in different waves of mass migration. According to historians, the first wave of migration occurred during the tenth century BCE from a region between the Yellow and Yangtze rivers in China. Clusters of ancient Naga settlements have been found around the Irrawaddy and Chindwin rivers in Burma (present-day Myanmar). Scholars believe that the ancient Nagas travelled through the Indo-Myanmar corridor and settled in Nagaland, Assam, Manipur and Arunachal Pradesh.

One of these tribes that settled in Phek district in the southeastern part of Nagaland is the Chakhesang tribe, which includes people belonging to three language groups—the Chokris, the Khezas and the Sangtams. Until the 1940s, the Chakhesangs were grouped with the Angamis, another major tribe of Nagaland and were known as the eastern Angamis because they inhabited the eastern parts of the Naga Hills. However, in 1946, the three language groups of the Chokris, the Khezas and the Sangtams integrated to form the Chakhesang tribe. After the recognition of the Sangtam tribe (now Pochury) as a separate tribe in 1990, it is no longer a part of the Chakhesang tribe.

The majority of the Chakhesang population is involved in agriculture. The tribe is known for its *jabo kheti* (terrace farming), a sustainable form of agriculture practised in the hilly terrain. Most farmers cultivate paddy, with over twenty varieties grown in the Chakhesang regions, along with corn, sesame, millets and different types of vegetables and pulses. For the Chakhesangs, farming and community life are so interconnected that many of their folk traditions have their origins in agricultural practices.

THE MEGALITH CULTURE OF THE CHAKHESANG NAGAS

The Chakhesangs, like many other Naga tribes, are a megalithic (mega = great; lithos = stone) people. Hundreds of standing stones can be found scattered across Nagaland. The purpose of erecting these megaliths varies among communities. While some megaliths have origins steeped in fantastic folklore, others are erected as part of rituals to display prosperity, gain recognition from society or signify important events such as death and birth.

Another important aspect of the Chakhesang life is their textile tradition. If you visit a Chakhesang village, you'll find racks of black-and-crimson shawls airing outside every house and skeins of colourful threads spread around women working on their back-strapped looms. These shawls are more than just garments; they are storied artifacts that embody the community's values and beliefs. Featuring linear, geometric designs, the shawls are tailored to specific age and gender groups, with certain patterns reserved exclusively for chieftains or influential clans that have a certain social standing.

Gaining influence within the clan involves a step-by-step process known as the Feast of Merit, each step marked by different rituals, foods, guest combinations and elaborate performances. The first step involves hosting a village feast to celebrate wealth and share good returns with the community. Completing the second step earns the right to place a wooden crossbeam on the eaves of one's house, with the ends tilting skyward above the roof. Upon completing the final step, one gains the right to erect commemorative stones in the village.

Like all Naga tribes, the Chakhesangs, for the longest time, had no tradition of written literature as literacy spread in Nagaland only towards the end of the nineteenth century. Although the Chakhesangs' relationship with the written word is relatively recent, their rich oral traditions have long served as a repository for their histories, languages, customs and beliefs. Central to these traditions is li, which embodies the timeless human need to share stories of joy, triumph and struggle, helping to define their identity.

SONGS OF THE PEOPLE

The Nagas have long been known for their love of music. It is believed that their Naga ancestors often communicated with each other through songs, using varied tunes and expressions. At a time when language had no written forms, people taught the younger ones to communicate through songs, which have always remained an integral part of the Naga life.

Agriculture is also intimately tied to music. One of the ways the Chakhesang farmers cultivate rice is by singing along. The splish-splosh sounds of the wet terrace fields in the villages of Phek district are often punctuated by songs sung by the farmers, both men and women. These songs, sung in the Chokri language, offer insights into the rural and cultural life of the Chakhesangs, their relationships with families, friends and the larger communities, as well as various social and political issues.

During peak cultivation seasons, Chakhesang farmers collaborate to plow, irrigate, plant, harvest and thresh each other's rice paddies. These cooperative agricultural groups are called *müle*. While they work, they sing together, synchronizing their songs to their physical movements. This choral singing of lis helps to reduce the tedium of physically demanding tasks and thus increases productivity. Apart from forging strong bonds within the agricultural group, lis also remind the farmers that they need each other to thrive—without each other, there would be no song.

Traditional li singing is based on the belief that it cannot be sung by a single voice. It requires a minimum of two voices and a maximum of eight. The choral voices in li are layered, with singers overlapping beats and harmonies. There are defined vocal parts for male and female performers, along with some interjecting melodies. While western choral music typically has four voice parts—soprano, alto, tenor and bass, li has six—*retsu, lishwu, lireh, liso, vathre* and *libo*. The melodies move up and down (and sometimes even sideways!), harmonizing perfectly through the use of intervals. Many lis employ a call-and-response style, resembling conversations between singers. The singers perform parts of the song to each other and, phrase by phrase, the song comes alive.

Lis are simple yet nuanced—the words are never quite what they mean and express a range of emotions and feelings. The lyrics follow a fixed verse structure with alternating lines, where the first line has four syllables and the second line has five. Derived largely from everyday activities of the community, there is a li for every occasion—songs about the breaking of clod and pulverizing soil in a field, sowing seeds, harvesting, pounding rice, lifting heavy loads, hunting and expressing gratitude for good health and youth. One such li, sung during the pulverization of soil in the field, goes something like this:

Hi-i ho-I . . . Hi-i ho-I.

Hülü-ü natsih, Hülü-ü natsih,

Hülü-ü natsih, Hülü-ü natsih.

Hizo ta-e ho-o le-ü,

Hizo ta-e ho-o le-ü.

Ho-o ha-e ho-o . . .

Hi zhale-ü ho-yi,

Ho-o hoh.

Hi-i ho-I, Hi-i ho-I,

Ho-o hi-ü ho-o he-ü.

Hi-i ho-I, Hi-i ho-i, hi-i-ho-I.

Uko-ü ta-e zho,

Uko-ü ta-e zho.

Mirüsa-ü mo-o le-ü,

Mirüsa-ü mo-o le-ü.

Ho-o ha-e ho-o,

Hi zhale-ü ho-yi.

Ho-o hoh.

Hi-i ho-I, Hi-i ho-I,

Ho-o hi-ü ho-o he-ü.

Hi-i ho-I, Hi-i ho-i, hi-i-ho-I.

[Hi-i ho-I . . . Hi-i ho-I (a li expression in Chokri that greets the listener, inviting them to sing).
We will not remain young (sung by the lead singer),
Will not remain young (sung by the followers).
Like this forever (sung by the lead singer),
Like this forever (sung by the followers).

If we are together (sung by the lead singer),
If we are together (sung by the followers).
We don't long for others (sung by the lead singer),
We don't long for others (sung by the followers).]

Since lis have been passed down orally for generations, the lyrics tend to be improvised. The singers might use one or two lines they've heard from others and then add some contextual lines based on their own experiences and emotions. In this way, people negotiate between the old and the new while maintaining the community-based tradition.

OF SOUNDS AND STRINGS

Li is often accompanied by the tunes of an indigenous musical instrument called the *libuh* or *heka libuh*. A one-stringed instrument similar to the ektara, it is about three to four feet in length and made from a dried, carved-out bottle gourd. The bottle gourd resonator is then covered with a thin film, traditionally made of animal skin and attached to a bamboo neck. A string is tied to the two ends of the bamboo neck over the thin film covering the gourd resonator. The string is plucked to produce two characteristic sounds, *ta* and *ti*, that provide a rhythmic accompaniment to the singer. So, forms of li that are accompanied by the libuh are often called *tati*. The instrument can be played by an individual or by a group, with each person playing their own libuh to create a harmonious ensemble.

SAME MUSIC. DIFFERENT FAITHS.

For the longest time, the Nagas were animists, believing that all things—from rocks and trees to animals and humans—possessed a spirit. They worshipped nature through songs and dances.

With the advent of Christianity in the nineteenth century, many Chakhesang Nagas adopted the new faith but faced the challenge of integrating their traditional practices with Christian teachings. Many of their folk music forms such as li were initially rejected since these songs did not align with the principles of church music. As a result, people stopped singing li.

However, at some point, the Chakhesangs realized that certain traditions, especially music, did not have to be abandoned because of religion. They began incorporating elements of the traditional li into Christian worship. One notable figure who infused gospel lyrics into Chakhesang music was Ethshiru from Chizami village in Phek district. Though the lyrics of the songs changed over time, their significance remained. Today, many of these ancient melodies are sung in churches, illustrating a creative synthesis.

There are several stories about how the libuh came into existence. A popular Chakhesang legend attributes the invention to a man who wanted to woo a woman. To express his love, he decided to sing a courting li called *nohu li*. He thought of using a musical instrument as an accompaniment to his singing. He saw a bottle gourd and decided to turn it into an instrument by carving it and tightening a string around it. He strummed the string with his fingernails as he sang to the woman he loved. Whether it turned out to be a tale with a happy ending or one about unrequited love remains uncertain.

The libuh gets its name from the bottle gourd. In the Chokri language, a *he* (flask), made from a bottle gourd, is called *he-buh*. Similarly, an instrument made of a bottle gourd to accompany li is called *li-buh*. Due to its fragility, the original libuh was prone to cracking when dropped. As a result, the more durable horn of a mithun or cow began to be used to create the resonator. The libuh that used animal horns came to be known as heka libuh.

For the neck pole of the libuh, a special kind of bamboo species called the *kuvwu* is used. Strong, straight and without holes, it is perfect for creating the pole. The carved bottle gourd resonator was traditionally covered with an animal bladder or a bamboo sheath. But the sounds produced by animal bladder varied as it tightened in dry weather. The bamboo sheath was also not very durable, so metal sheets came to be used to cover the resonator. Originally, the strings of the instrument were woven from the bark of certain trees or strong cotton threads, conditioned using rice starch. Now, metal strings are used instead.

THE SINGING SISTERS

One interesting aspect of folk music is its timelessness—
it is never truly new or old. It is rooted in the everyday
experiences of a community, yet it can change with every
rendition. The Tetseo Sisters, a band of four Chakhesang
Naga siblings, embody this by melding the folk melodies of
li with modern influences.

Born and raised in Kohima, the band consists of four
sisters—Mütselü (Mercy), Azine (Azi), Kuvelü (Kuku)
and Alüne Tetseo (Lulu). They are often accompanied
by their guitarist and music-producer brother Mhaseve.
Originally from the village of Thuvopisu in Phek district,
their parents introduced them to various forms of music,
especially li from their home region. Like most people in
Nagaland, they grew up listening to music and singing at
home, school and church choirs.

For the Tetseo sisters, their musical journey began
when they sang a li taught to them by their mother for
a cultural festival in school, which led to an opportunity
to sing for the Doordarshan annual day. They recorded
a couple of programmes that were broadcast on repeat,
helping the siblings gain national attention and take the
first steps toward building a music career. They formally
came together as Tetseo Sisters in 1994 and have since
performed all over the country.

The sibling quartet sings li in the Chokri dialect.
While they retain the original melodies of the songs, they
work with the verses to incorporate more contemporary
themes. Wearing traditional Naga costumes, including
wrap-around skirts known as *phanek*, tribal jewellery and

elaborate headgear and using indigenous instruments such as libuh and *khrokhro* (a gourd shaker filled with beads that bears a resemblance to the tambourine), they sing about love, seasons, friendship, nature, peace, war, life and death. Between songs, they explain the meaning of each piece and why they perform li. Sometimes, at their concert venues, they also curate mini exhibits with photographs and hand-written letters that bring alive the stories of the Chakhesangs.

The band officially debuted with an album called *Li Chapter One: The Beginning* at the Hornbill Festival, the ten-day annual cultural fest of Nagaland that showcases the rich and diverse Naga tribes, in 2011. Apart from the traditional li, the Tetseo sisters also perform folk fusion and western music, K-pop collaborations and even hip-hop-tinged protest pop.

The Tetseo Sisters are cultural ambassadors who have brought li to a larger audience outside Nagaland. They have been introducing people to this musical form by bringing folk into conversation with the contemporary, while also preserving one of India's endangered languages, Chokri—one li at a time.

KNOTS IN HISTORY

The histories written in broad strokes by colonizers, victors and those in power have conveniently overlooked, purposefully removed or simply forgotten indigenous communities, particularly from the northeastern parts of India. The Chakhesang Nagas are one of many indigenous communities often omitted from accounts of our collective past.

Many of us are unfamiliar with Chakhesang Naga history and even when we have some knowledge, we often miss the depth of their stories. To truly understand their history, we must delve into their folk traditions. The strength of Chakhesang folk music tradition lies in its deep-rooted connection to the people it represents. In the intricate melodies of lis, we uncover the rich narratives of the community's origins and identity.

While we cannot undo how history was written in the past, what we can do is celebrate the marginalized microhistories of our country and attune ourselves to the distinct rhythms of their folk traditions.

LISTENING LIST:

Search words: Li, Libuh, Chakhesang Folk Songs, Chokri Folk Songs, Tetseo Sisters

1. 'O Rhosi', a li performed by the Tetseo Sisters, uses the indigenous rhosi flower of Nagaland as a metaphor for youth and vitality.
   https://www.youtube.com/watch?v=BmgWEBSTIYc

2. 'Chüte Li', a traditional Chakhesang folk song celebrating the millet sowing season.
   https://www.youtube.com/watch?v=lzjMyOzEVml

3. A video interview with Pusazo Venyo, a Chokri linguist and member of the Chokri Cultural Research Institute, and Kuvesho Tetseo, a prominent figure in the music and cultural world of the Chokri Chakhesang Nagas, discussing li and libuh.
   https://www.youtube.com/watch?v=74iCqiokIPA

4. A Chakhesang love song performed in the paddy fields of Thenyizumi village of Phek district.
   https://www.youtube.com/watch?v=hXAwlPNSopw

5. Tetseo Sisters performing a li at the Hornbill Festival 2013.
   https://www.youtube.com/watch?v=7ijkTAYdUSg

SONGS OF THE ETERNAL RIVER

The Bhatiyali Music of Bengal

Where there is a river, there are people living on its banks, boats travelling on its waters and the boatmen singing beautiful songs of the river. The long-drawn melodies of these songs wend their way through the rivers in West Bengal and Bangladesh, carrying stories of the lone journey of a majhi *(boatman).*

Aamay Bhashaili re, aamay doobaili re.

Okool duriaar boojhi, kul nai re . . .

Kul nai kinaar nai, nai ko suriaar paari,

Shaabdhane challiyo majhi, aamar bhanga tori re . . .

[You have set me afloat, you're causing me to drown.

This unfathomable river seems to have no end,

No banks, no bounds, no way to reach the shore . . .

O boatman, steer the boat cautiously,

This tattered boat of mine with its broken rim.]

A classic example of folk songs sung by boatmen in the eastern parts of India, this song—and many others sung in the region—portrays the rivers and the lives of people connected to them. Born out of an immense familiarity with the river and all its moods, these river songs are not always full of praise for the river. Instead, they form a candid dialogue with it, expressing pains and sorrows, complaints and questions, longings and, sometimes, even curses! The rivers are so intrinsically linked to the lives and livelihoods of those around them that they inspire the lyrics and structure of these songs. The river becomes a metaphor for the journey of life, the boat for a human and the oarsman for the divine being who guides one through the stream of life.

Unique in their form, music, words and spirit, these songs are one of the distinctive folk music traditions of eastern India and magically transport listeners to a riverside. This folk music tradition is known as *bhatiyali*.

A RIVERINE FOLK CULTURE

The world's greatest civilizations began next to great rivers—the Nile in north Africa, the Indus in the Indian subcontinent, the Tigris and the Euphrates in Mesopotamia. Rivers provided drinking water and fertile ground for cultivating crops. Early humans fished the shallows and hunted the birds and animals drawn to the waters. It was probably fishing from hollowed-out logs that led to the invention of boats and helped early humans increase their mobility. Since rivers traversed borders, they formed a network of waterway trade routes that contributed to the exchange of goods and ideas among diverse cultures.

In addition to shaping civilizations, rivers have deeply influenced cultural expressions, including music. From the ancient hymns of the Rigveda, composed around 1500 BCE, to modern chartbusters, rivers have inspired diverse musical forms. Bhatiyali belongs to this universal tradition.

Bengal's geography, stretching from the snowy Himalayas to the Bay of Bengal, is threaded with numerous rivers. Before it was partitioned by the British in the early twentieth century, it was a large province, the eastern part of which was broadly referred to as East Bengal (present-day Bangladesh). The eastern and western parts of Bengal, along with some parts of present-day Bihar, Assam and Tripura shared cultural bonds based on commonalities of language. This vast region is crisscrossed with multiple rivers—Ganga, Bhagirathi, Ajoy, Padma, Brahmaputra, Kabotaksha, Meghna, Madhumati and Biruganga—and it is here that the bhatiyali was born.

Although there is no record to indicate exactly when bhatiyali came into being, the classical form can be traced back to *Sreekrishna Kirtana*, a collection of devotional songs and poems written by Boru-Chandidas in the fifteenth century, where Lord Krishna is described as a boatman in one of the collection's thirteen sections. *Sekha Subhodgaya*, a sixteenth-century Sanskrit text that recounts the arrival of the celebrated Sufi saint Shaikh Jalaluddin Tabrizi in Bengal in the thirteenth century, shortly after the beginning of Muslim rule in India, mentions folk songs that are thematically similar to the bhatiyali.

The word 'bhatiyali' is derived from *bhata* (low tide). This is a period of slack water, during which the banks of the river become wider. The boatmen leave their oars and rely on the winds to direct their journeys, surrendering to the forces of nature to determine their destiny. It is from this philosophy that bhatiyali music emerged—slow-paced, much like the ebbs of the river. Scholars believe that the regions of Mymensingh, Sylhet, Dhaka and Rangpur in East Bengal (now Bangladesh) along the Brahmaputra river of the *bhati* (lower region of a river) were the more specific places where bhatiyali originated.

Traditionally, bhatiyali was composed and sung by the boatmen of Bengal whose existence revolved around the mighty rivers. These rivers brought the Bengal delta to life and provided its people with one of the cheapest forms of transport. Thus, majhis were an important part of daily life. Each village had a dock with a designated majhi. The majhi did not charge money for his services but was compensated in kind throughout the year. At the end of each harvest season, the majhi would receive a small share of every farmer's produce. The communities believed that if they did not share their produce with the majhi, then when the time came to cross the river of life, the supreme boatman or god would not help them.

When majhis went on long trips, they could become stranded for days or even months within the Ganga-Brahmaputra delta. Isolated from their families, they had to continuously ply their oars to stay on course. This prolonged solitude nurtured their imagination, leading them to ponder deep philosophical questions: Where did we come from and where would we go? Where will the river of life take us? Who is the oarsman holding the oars of the boat of our lives? For the majhis, the ever-flowing river became an inspiration for songs that reflected these existential dilemmas.

THE SONGS OF SOLITUDE

There is a rich variety of work-related songs in many Indian folk music traditions, including those of potters, oil-pressers, basket-makers, coppersmiths and roof-builders. Bhatiyali is also part of this tradition of

---

BOAT SONGS AROUND THE WORLD

The river and the boat have long been sources of musical inspiration across the globe. The songs of the Chuanjiang Haozi, originating along the Yangtze river in China, have been sung for centuries. These songs, typically led by a solo singer with others joining in, feature a repetitive tempo that helps synchronize rowing and eases the tedium of the task.

Perhaps the most famous boat song is the 'Song of the Volga Boatmen', with its iconic 'heave-ho' refrain. This traditional Russian folk song was originally sung by the Burlaks, the men who pulled barges upstream on the Volga river in the former USSR. The song not only provided the strength to endure their gruelling work but also served as a tribute to Mother Volga.

In the United States, the masterpiece 'Ol' Man River' was first performed in the 1927 musical *Show Boat*, portraying the hardships of African Americans working as dock labourers on the Mississippi river. The song gained further prominence when the celebrated singer and activist Paul Robeson performed it in the 1936 film adaptation, transforming it into a powerful anthem for Black liberation in the twentieth century. This rendition inspired many artists, including the renowned Indian musician Dr Bhupen Hazarika, who reimagined the song from an Indian perspective, creating the classic 'Bistirno Dupare', later translated into Hindi as 'Ganga Behti Ho Kyun'.

In central Kerala, *vanchipattu* are traditional boat songs, typically sung during religious ceremonies and snake-boat races, accompanied by traditional percussion instruments. Bengal also has a similar form of folk music called *sari*, often performed at boat races.

The Koli community of Maharashtra boasts a rich tradition of boat songs that accompany their lively dances, depicting various fishing activities such as rowing, casting nets and mimicking wave-like motions with swaying oars.

In Kashmir, the boatmen known as *hanjis* have their own tradition of boat songs, called *hainzbaith*, adding yet another unique voice to the global chorus of river-inspired music.

work songs. However, it stands apart as it is sung not only by boatmen but also by farmers tilling their land, shepherds returning home after grazing their cattle and fishermen casting their nets far and wide. Unlike other work songs that aid community work, bhatiyali serves as a means of personal reflection. One can imagine these songs echoing through the woods and meadows by the river. Occasionally, other boatmen would hear the songs and join in, continuing the melody from where it left off.

Bhatiyali songs are not very rhythmic and are typically sung without any accompaniment. The singer's loud, full-throated voice alone is central to this music form. Most bhatiyali songs have long, drawn-out notes, starting with high-pitched tones and gradually settling into lower ones. This allows listeners to easily follow the variations in pitch. Structurally, bhatiyali is always short and simple.

The first verse of the bhatiyali songs is referred to as *ujan* (upstream) and the second verse as *bhaital* (downstream). The lyrics reflect the journey of the boatman travelling down the vast, seemingly endless river. The poignancy of the lyrics often lies in their dual meanings, where boats symbolize bodies, lovers represent lost gods and riverbanks stand for cycles of life and death. Throughout, the melody, with its tonal variations, vividly portrays riverine life in Bengal.

THE GOLDEN ERA OF BHATIYALI

Long before we could ask Alexa to play our favourite song or find it on Spotify, gramophone records and radio dominated the audio world. In 1902, the Gramophone

BHATIYALI, BAUL AND BHAWAIYA

Bengal's folk music spans a wide spectrum of genres, from secular songs to religious hymns, social ballads to workmen's chants, protest anthems to narrative songs based on myths and legends, reflecting its cultural diversity.

The best-known folk music traditions of Bengal are bhatiyali, *bhawaiya* and *baul*. Bhawaiya is the music of *gariyals* (bullock-cart drivers) and *mahishals* (buffalo keepers). Sung to the tune of *dotara*, a four-stringed lute, bhawaiya is said to have originated in north Bengal. The name comes from the word *bhav* (emotion) and it is believed to have developed from the theatrical musical form *pala gaan*, which was once the mainstay of rural entertainment. These songs express a range of emotions, including love and loneliness.

Baul represents a tradition of devotional songs influenced by the Bhakti movement, Sufi music traditions and Buddhism. The word 'baul' originated from the Sanskrit words *vatula* (mad) or *vyakula* (restless), describing those in a fervent quest for god. The bauls—both men and women—are wandering mystics who reject traditional societal norms. They earn their living from singing to the accompaniment of an ektara, a simple one-stringed instrument, and a *dubki* (drum).

Company in London sent recording experts to explore different countries and cultures, capturing their music. Their arrival in India had far-reaching social and musical effects as vocal and instrumental music reached a mass audience for the first time. Prior to the gramophone, people could only enjoy live performances, but gramophone allowed them to listen to music in the comfort of their homes. It enabled people from one part of the country to experience music from another, making gramophone an instant hit and an integral part of every Indian household.

Over the next few decades, regional Indian music gained popularity nationwide. Recording companies began to view folk songs as a commercial opportunity. By the 1930s, folk songs had captivated audiences in both big cities and small towns. Soon, the radio started featuring folk singers for short performances, occasionally bringing groups from remote villages to offer city audiences a taste of authentic folk songs. The melodious bhatiyali songs began to capture hearts across Bengal and beyond.

One prominent figure in popularizing bhatiyali was Abbasuddin Ahmed. Born in Balarampur in the district of Cooch Bihar (now in West Bengal) in 1901, Abbasuddin spent his early years immersed in the music of the countryside. He was captivated by the bhawaiya songs of buffalo cart drivers and the mesmerizing strains of their dotara. Self-taught Abbasuddin began performing the folk songs he had heard as a child. Initially famous for his bhawaiya renditions, he later gained acclaim for his bhatiyali songs, including the notable 'Aamay Bhashaili Re'. Abbasuddin became a leading figure in Bengali folk music, recording approximately seven hundred songs and inspiring several other folk singers such as Abdul Alim, Sohrab Hossain, Bedaruddin Ahmed, Kanai Lal Sheel, Nayeb Ali Lepu, Abdul Latif, Osman Khan and Mumtaj Ali Khan.

Nirmalendu Chowdhury also brought Bengali folk music, especially bhatiyali, to international audiences. His powerful voice on radio and gramophone records became immensely popular in the post-independence Calcutta (now Kolkata), capturing the hearts of a whole generation. In 1955, he performed at the Grand Bolshoi Theatre in Moscow and later won a gold medal at an international folk song convention in Warsaw. Over his career, he performed in over twenty countries across four continents, popularizing bhatiyali globally.

In Indian films, bhatiyali songs were used to evoke specific moods, particularly in the films from the 1930s to the 1960s, which is considered the golden era of bhatiyali music. Sachin Dev Burman, a renowned music composer, redefined Hindi film music by incorporating folk tunes from the banks of the Gomti river in Comilla

BHATIYALI AND CLIMATE CHANGE

Long before the term 'climate change' became popular in the 1970s, bhatiyali singers were documenting its impacts through their songs. These folk melodies have long addressed issues such as the receding waters of rivers, seasonal upheavals, and their effects on livelihoods. Many bhatiyali songs reflect on the changing environment and offer insights into how communities have historically navigated climate distress.

(now Bangladesh). From a young age, Sachin had a keen ear for music, walking miles into rural Bengal to listen to minstrels or sitting by rivers to hear the songs of boatmen and fishermen. When he began composing music for Hindi films in Mumbai, he sought to recreate the rhythms of his childhood. He blended elements of bhatiyali with Indian classical music and, later, western classical music, to create some memorable songs such as 'Sun Mere Bandhu Re' (*Sujata*, 1959), 'Mere Saajan Hai Uss Paar' *(Bandini*, 1963) and 'Wahan Kaun Hai Tera' (*Guide*, 1965).

Over the decades, folk music has increasingly mixed with contemporary genres like pop and rock. Today, popular bands in India and Bangladesh experiment with bhatiyali folk tunes, blending them with modern music to bring out unique combinations of sounds, beats and melodies. With the digital transformation and platforms like Coke Studio, this new sound is finding fresh audiences. Although transformed, bhatiyali continues to reach people around the world.

RIVERS OF LIFE

Every river carries with it a rich tapestry of stories, songs, myths, legends, festivals and rituals born along its banks. These riverine cultures transcend religion and national boundaries. Bhatiyali, a living link between the rivers of Bengal and its people, is one such riverine folk tradition.

However, this tradition is slowly fading. Over the past century, nearly seven hundred rivers in the Ganga-Brahmaputra delta in Bengal and the Padma and Meghna in Bangladesh have disappeared—many now buried under asphalt streets or city gutters. The remaining rivers are strained by overexploitation and many are on the brink of extinction. As bhatiyali music is deeply connected to its natural surroundings, its repertoire is gradually diminishing, with no new songs being added.

Despite the dire situation, our rivers possess remarkable resilience. There is still hope for their revival and with them, our riverine folk cultures can flourish once again, their songs echoing through generations to remind us of the enduring bond between nature and humanity.

LISTENING LIST:

Search words: Bhatiyali Folk Music, Songs of the Boatmen, Abbasuddin Ahmed, Nirmelendu Chowdhury, Alamgir, Fariha Pervez, Sachin Dev Burman, River Songs

1. The bhatiyali song 'Aamay Bhashaili Re' by Abbasuddin Ahmed.
   https://www.youtube.com/watch?v=vwmx1Keh7tg

2. A contemporary rendition of the bhatiyali song 'Aamay Bhashaili Re' by Alamgir and Fariha Pervez, featured on Coke Studio Pakistan.
   https://www.youtube.com/watch?v=FnDmg-cBVsA

3. The bhatiyali folk song 'Bandure Akule Bhasaiya', sung by Nirmalendu Chowdhury.
   https://www.youtube.com/watch?v=cTBOxKxzq_O

4. 'Sun Mere Bandhu Re', a timeless classic from the movie Sujata, beautifully composed by Sachin Dev Burman.
   https://www.youtube.com/watch?v=g9eppdrcyHI

5. A boatman sings 'Majhi Baya Jaao Re' as he glides along a river.
   https://www.youtube.com/watch?app=desktop&v=yYjYLpd200g

LET THE MUSIC PLAY ON!

Folk music in India, deeply rooted in the everyday lives of ordinary people, continues to thrive across many communities. However, the material conditions that sustain these traditions are under pressure and many communities are struggling to keep their musical heritage alive. Recent archival efforts have been crucial in revitalizing these traditions, documenting invaluable songs—especially among marginalized communities—and preserving them for future generations. It would be remiss not to acknowledge these important initiatives.

If you wish to continue your folk music adventure—and we hope you do—you might find these efforts particularly useful.

1. The Bidesia Project
   https://www.youtube.com/channel/UC2jnfWIA9dtN6__bDD9HhpQ

2. Rupayan Sansthan and Arna Jharna Museum
   https://www.youtube.com/@Kuldeeparna

3. The Ladishah Project
   http://www.ladishahproject.org/

4. PARI Network
   https://ruralindiaonline.org/en/gallery/categories/audiozone/

5. Urban Folk Project
   https://www.projectanywhere.net/urban-folk-project/

6. The Kabir Project
   https://ajabshahar.com/about

7. The Qawwali Project
   https://www.youtube.com/
   playlist?list=PLFEdHLPTgJoivnITK-toHF4A4a-6ChJtg

8. The Music Academy, Chennai
   https://musicacademymadras.in/explore/the-music-academy-tag-digital-archives/

9. Uramili Project
   https://www.youtube.com/@uramili

10. The Travelling Archive
    https://www.thetravellingarchive.org/home/

BIBLIOGRAPHY

Chand, Satish. 'Socio-Political Consequences of Forced Migration: The Case of Indian Indentured Workers to Fiji.' *Studia Historica Gednanensia*, vol. 5, no. 1: 139–153 (2014). http://www.ejournals. eu/sj/index.php/SHG/article/viewFile/4709/4569 (accessed 25 September, 2024).

Allen, Richard. 'Capital, Illegal Slaves, Indentured Labourers and the Creation of a Sugar Plantation Economy in Mauritius, 1810–60.' *The Journal of Imperial and Commonwealth History*, vol. 36, no. 2: 151–170 (2008). https://doi.org/10.1080/03086530802180569 (accessed 25 September, 2024).

Gillion, Kenneth. *Fiji's Indian Migrants: A History to the End of Indenture in 1920.* Oxford: Oxford University Press, 1962.

Kire, Easterine. *Walking the Roadless Road: Exploring the Tribes of Nagaland.* New Delhi: Aleph Book Company, 2019.

Thakur, Bhikhari. *Rachnavali.* Edited by Ram Bajhawan Singh and Mithilesh Kumari Mishra. Bihar: Bihar Rashtrabhasha Parishad, 2011.

Mishra, Abhinav. 'Bidesia by Bhikhari Thakur: The Play which Shaped the Playwright and the Playwright Who Shaped Bhojpuri History.' Paper, JNU (2021). https://www.academia.edu/69477936/Bidesia_by_ Bhikhari_Thakur_edited_1_ (accessed 25 September, 2024).

Sridharan, D.V. *Good News India: Ordinary Indians, Extraordinary Triumphs.* New Delhi: Bloomsbury India, 2021.

Konishi, Kodai. 'Phantasm in Lime: The Permeating Modernity in Manganiyar Community of Rajasthan.' *International Journal of South Asian Studies*, vol. 7 (2015). https://jasas.info/wp-content/themes/ jasas/pdf/relevance/ijsas_vol07/177_Kodai-Konishi.pdf (accessed 25 September, 2024).

Singh, Khushwant. 'Extinction of Afghan Power in Northern India.' In *A History of the Sikhs,* edited by H.L.O. Garrett. Oxford: Oxford University Press, 1918.

Smith, David. *The First Anglo-Sikh War*. Oxford: Osprey Publishing, 2019.

Puri, Balraj. *Kashmir Towards Insurgency*. New Delhi: Orient Blackswan, 1993.

Desmond, Edward. 'The Insurgency in Kashmir (1989–1991).' *Contemporary South Asia*, vol. 4, no. 1: 5-16 (1995). Available at Taylor and Francis, https://doi.org/10.1080/09584939508719748.

Upadhyay, Bela. *'One Who Serves Becomes the Master': Life Lessons from Hazrat Nizamuddin*. New Delhi: Aleph Book Company, 2021.

Parveen, Babli. 'The Eclectic Spirit of Sufism in India: An Appraisal.' *Social Scientist* vol. 42, no. 11 & 12 (2014). https://www.jstor.org/stable/i24372895 (accessed 25 September, 2024).

Nizami, Sadia. 'Sufi Saints of India: The Role of Hazrat Nizamuddin Aulia in Indian Nation Building.' *Journal of Emerging Technologies and Innovative Research*, vol. 8 no. 11 (2021). https://www.jetir.org/papers/JETIR2111286.pdf (accessed 25 September, 2024).

Lawrence, Bruce B., trans. and annotated. *Nizam Ad-Din Awliya: Morals of the Heart*. New York: Paulist Press, 2017.

Joshi, G. N. 'A Concise History of the Phonograph Industry in India.' *Popular Music*, vol. 7, no. 2: 147–56 (1988). http://www.jstor.org/stable/853533 (accessed 25 September, 2024).

Vadukut, Sidin. 'Finding the First Indian Recording in the Gramophone Company's 19th-Century Catalogue.' Mint, 9 June 2017. Available at livemint.com, https://www.livemint.com/Leisure/kKa839pmjIXkyj8vn67K9H/Finding-the-first-Indian-recording-in-The-Gramophone-Company.html.

Mudgal, Shubha. 'Coloured notes.' Mint, 9 March 2012. Available at livemint.com, https://www.livemint.com/Leisure/LiVrb1jszdyZ36Enx2Zw5L/Coloured-notes.html.

Kibria, Shahwar. 'How Amir Khusrau's 'Rung' Inspired the Film and Music Culture of South Asia.' Firstpost, 26 November 2017. Available at firstpost.com, https://www.firstpost.com/living/how-amir-khusraus-rung-inspired-the-film-and-music-culture-of-south-asia-4228239.html.

Singh, Anita. *Staging Feminisms: Gender, Violence and Performance in Contemporary India*. New Delhi: Routledge India, 2021.

Kumari, Barkha. 'Strings of the Past.' Bangalore Mirror, 28 January 2018. Available at bangaloremirror.indiatimes.com, https://bangaloremirror. indiatimes.com/opinion/sunday-read/strings-of-the-past/ articleshow/62676242.cms.

Sayeed, Vikhar Ahmed. 'The Padma Shri for Manjamma Jogathi Does Her, Her Community and Karnataka Proud.' Frontline, 19 February 2021. Available at frontline.thehindu.com, https://frontline.thehindu.com/ arts-and-culture/the-padma-shri-for-manjamma-jogathi-does-her-her-community-and-karnataka-proud/article33872818.ece.

Jogathi, B. Manjamma, and Harsha Bhat. *Manjunath to Manjamma: The Inspiring Life of a Transgender Folk Artist*. Gurugram: HarperCollins India, 2023.

Rashid, Atikh. 'Know Your City: Bavankhani, A 'Place of Pleasure' in Peshwa-era Pune.' *The Indian Express*, 24 October 2021. https:// indianexpress.com/article/cities/pune/know-your-city-bavankhani-a-place-of-pleasure-in-peshwa-era-pune-7586166/.

Tiwade, Kavita, and Salama Maner. 'Unheard Voice of Subaltern in Kishore Shantabai Kale's Against All Odds.' *Vivek Research Journal*, Special Issue (2022).

Bansode, Rupali. 'The Linked Caste Slavery of the Kolhatis and the Bedias.' Round Table India, 29 April 2014. https://www.roundtableindia.co.in/ the-linked-caste-slavery-of-the-kolhatis-and-the-bedias/.

Gogoi, Akhil Kumar. 'A Study of the Immigration of Nagas to North-East India and Their Present Location (With Special Reference to Nagaland).' *PalArch's Journal of Archaeology of Egypt/Egyptology*, vol. 17 no.12: 1141–46 (2020). https://archives.palarch.nl/index.php/jae/ article/view/6636 (accessed 25 September 2024).

Mishra, Kaveri. 'Naga Agitation: How One of India's Oldest Insurgencies Started.' Outlook, 29 August 2022. Available at outlookindia.com, https://www.outlookindia.com/national/naga-agitation-how-one-of-india-s-oldest-insurgencies-started-news-219529.

Agarwala, Tora. 'How Naga Chants Came to Set the Rhythm for a Musical.' *The Indian Express*, 19 December 2018. https://indianexpress.com/article/north-east-india/nagaland/first-a-tribal-chant-then-a-world-music-genre-and-now-a-film-5499397/.

Konyak, Manpa, and Paromita Das. 'The Folk Songs and Performances of Eastern Nagas: The Bedrock of Social Communication and Development.' *Communicator*, vol. 13, no. 3: 1–9 (2023). https://www.researchgate.net/publication/377895039_The_Folk_Songs_and_Performances_of_Eastern_Nagas_The_Bedrock_of_Social_Communication_and_Development (accessed 25 September, 2024).

Mamta Nainy is a writer based in New Delhi. She
has authored over thirty-five books for children,
many of which have won national and international
awards, including Valley of Words Awards 2022, FICCI
Publishing Awards 2022, Publishing Next Award 2022,
The Hindu Young World-Goodbooks Award 2019 and
Peek-a-Book Children's Choice Award 2019. She also
works as a literary translator, translating between
Hindi and English. She is inspired by the boundless
imagination of children and loves to travel but is often
too lazy to do so—so she mostly makes do with reading.

Read More in the Series

10 INDIAN ART MYSTERIES THAT HAVE NEVER BEEN SOLVED

MAMTA NAINY

This book tells the stories of ten mysterious people, styles and objects in Indian art from the prehistoric period to the present day-and in the process, it captures some of the diversity and range of the very large canvas we call Indian art. The stories told here include those of:

The Bhimbetka paintings

The evolution of the Buddha

The Ajanta caves

The Kailashanatha temple

The Pithora paintings

Women artists of the Mughal era

Bani Thani Indian yellow

Manaku of Guler

The Sripuranthan

Shiva Nataraja

Mamta Nainy explores diverse artistic periods, explains different art forms, and gives insights into the lives of artists working in different times and spaces, one curious case at a time.

Read More in the Series

10 INDIAN TRIBES AND THE UNIQUE LIVES THEY LEAD

NIDHI DUGAR KUNDALIA

This book tells the story of ten Indian tribes who have been living lives very different—far away from or even within the same physical spaces—from the rest of mainstream India. Their histories have seldom been told. These tribes are . . .

The Halakkis

The Konyak Nagas

The Alu Kurumbas

The Hill Marias

The Meos

The Kanjars

The Changpas

The Khasis

The Jarawa

The Bhils

Nidhi Dugar Kundalia traces the origins and explores the customs, religious practices, beliefs and daily lives of some of the many tribes who share the country with us.